Learn Chinese
Without
WRITING 3
The Chinese Spelling Book

W.Q. BLOSH

Learn Chinese Without Writing 3
The Chinese Spelling Book
W.Q. BLOSH

FIRST EDITION

Written and designed by W.Q. BLOSH

Email: wqblosh@gmail.com
Website: http://www.learnchinesewithoutwriting.com/

ISBN: 978-981-11-1651-3

Printed by IngramSparks

PREFACE

Congratulations! You have come to Step 3 of *Learn Chinese Without Writing* (LCWW). LCWW3 rounds up the theory part on LCWW and provides you with the third set of tips on how to 'see' patterns in Chinese characters. With these three books, you will feel confident to decode any *simplified Chinese characters* during your learning journey.

In this book, you will learn to see patterns through **structures** . In LCWW2, the 'Chinese Alphabets Book', you learnt the qTRAILS alphabets; in LCWW3, the *'Chinese Spelling Book'*, you will learn how to 'spell' (construct) Chinese characters.

In contrast to English words which are always spelt from left to right, Chinese characters have more than a dozen types of basic structures. When these structures are combined to form complex structures, there is a myriad of possibilities. Hence beginners get more confused the more characters they learn.

If you still have the mindset that you need to practise writing every Chinese character individually in your mind, it is time to transcend such thinking. After you have learnt to interpret them visually, you will be surprised to discover that there are so many common patterns within Chinese characters. Our radical approach is a more productive and system-atic way to remember Chinese characters visually.

As in the two previous books, this book will not teach you the meaning and pronunciation of characters. We believe that developing the ability to see will benefit you more in the long run. In fact, we hope that you will be able to have a helicopter view of the characters you are going to encounter during your learning journey. The remaining rare characters that you encounter once in a blue moon will be as simple as ABC to you after you have developed the ability to see.

Most of you probably have interacted with LCWW1 and LCWW2 before coming to this book, then you are very familiar with the new terminologies we have introduced in this series of books. In fact, you have overcome the more difficult hurdles by now. With LCWW3, you will be able to see the big picture by incorporating what you have learnt in the first two books (see next page).

If you have missed out LCWW1 and/or LCWW2, you will be able to get the key ideas in the recap sections. Skipping the recap sections will make your learning more tedious as you may have to refer back to these pages frequently. The priority is to learn the 35 strokes and the 32 Stroke Patterns first.

Find out where to get LCWW1 and 2 on page 223.

WARNING
Please DO NOT attempt to memorise all the characters in this book.

We want to expose you to as many varied characters that you are likely to come across (we are confident that we have a good coverage of the characters).

The key purpose is to get you to enter the flow state—the auto-pilot mode that you will experience when you are proficient. Build your confidence to do self-directed learning.

Again, remember the purpose is not to memorise the characters, the purpose is to 'SEE'—what we have stressed since LCWW1.

3 Easy Steps
TO LEARN CHINESE

STEP 3

STEP 2

STEP 1
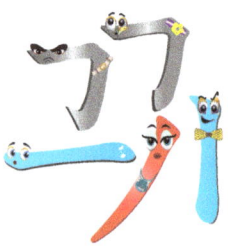

 **LEARNING**

Structures
Part Order

Alphabets
Stroke Order

Strokes
Stroke Flow

DECODING

 LEARNING

When you are learning, you start from Step 1. In LCWW1 you learnt the 35 strokes; in LCWW2 you learnt how to combine these strokes to form qTRAILS Alphabets according to the 32 Stroke Patterns. Now in this book you will learn how to combine alphabets and/or strokes to form characters according to some simple rules.

DECODING

When you are applying what you have learnt, you start from the opposite direction from Step 3. You analyse the structures of characters and decode them into alphabets and/or strokes. The alphabets could be further broken down into the basic strokes.

WHY THIS BOOK

Many beginners see Chinese characters as a stack of intersecting strokes and are unable to see patterns that can be systematically remembered and retrieved easily when needed.

LINE VERSUS SQUARE

As discussed in LCWW1, learning Chinese characters could be disorienting for foreign learners who are used to writing words linearly from left to right. Instead of spacing each alphabet equally on a horizontal line, **strokes** of a Chinese character are **spread across a square** artistically.

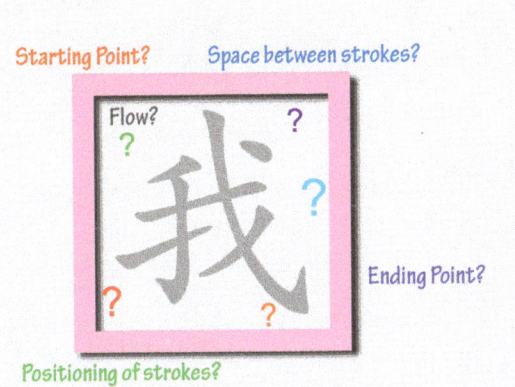

Where should the starting point be?

Which stroke does it end with?

How to flow from one stroke to another?

How to position the strokes in the box?

INADEQUATE GUIDELINES ON STROKE ORDER

Stroke order guidelines on how to write Chinese characters can be found in textbooks. They are usually written as *'When you see...then write this first/last'.* However these guidelines are not sufficient for beginners and may even make them more confused. Some of the reasons are:

* These gudelines are general advice that are applicable only to characters with simple structures.

* There are exceptions to the guidelines and hence may confuse beginners.

* Often these guidelines are explained in words and not presented visually hence more difficult for learners to remember visually.

The guidelines are short and crisp and easy to recite in Mandarin but when they are translated into English, the sentences become longer and lose the short-and-sweet characteristics that Mandarin speakers appreciate. As a result, non-native learners perceive these guidelines very differently from native-speakers, finding them difficult to visualise and remember.

See page 6 for more explanation.

PLAY TO LEARN CHINESE

It has always been difficult to not write to learn Chinese characters and there are limited ways to play Chinese words like Scrabble or Crossword. One reason is that characters are not reorganised for easy dismantling and construction. In this book, you will learn to decode Chinese characters by their structures and not by strokes. Now Chinese characters are seen as square boxes that can be broken into blocks, strips, L-frame, 7-frame, etc. Hence, you can imagine playing Chinese characters... it is like playing Brickgame, Lego or Tetris. In these games, there are components that can be put together in different ways to create different formations. Learning Chinese characters is more challenging than these games because

* There are more formations (patterns) to remember
* There are many similar-looking formations that need to be distinguished carefully
* Characters can be further broken down into smaller components—alphabets and strokes
* The sequence of the components in characters is important

To play the Chinese characters game, beginners will need to find a systematic way to remember the components—**alphabets** (covered in LCWW2) and **strokes** (covered in LCWW1). Now, in LCWW3 you will learn how to 'play' with these parts and put them together.

WHICH IS THE STARTING POINT?

The Starting Point

The general guideline on the starting point of a Chinese character is that it falls within one of the shaded boxes (see diagram) in a square box divided into 3 by 3 grids.

With this general guideline, would you be able to pinpoint the starting point of these Chinese characters?

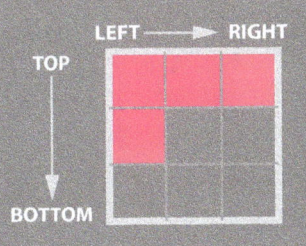

Guess which is the starting point?
Is it the highest point of the character?
Or the leftmost point of the character?
Decide on your answers before moving on.

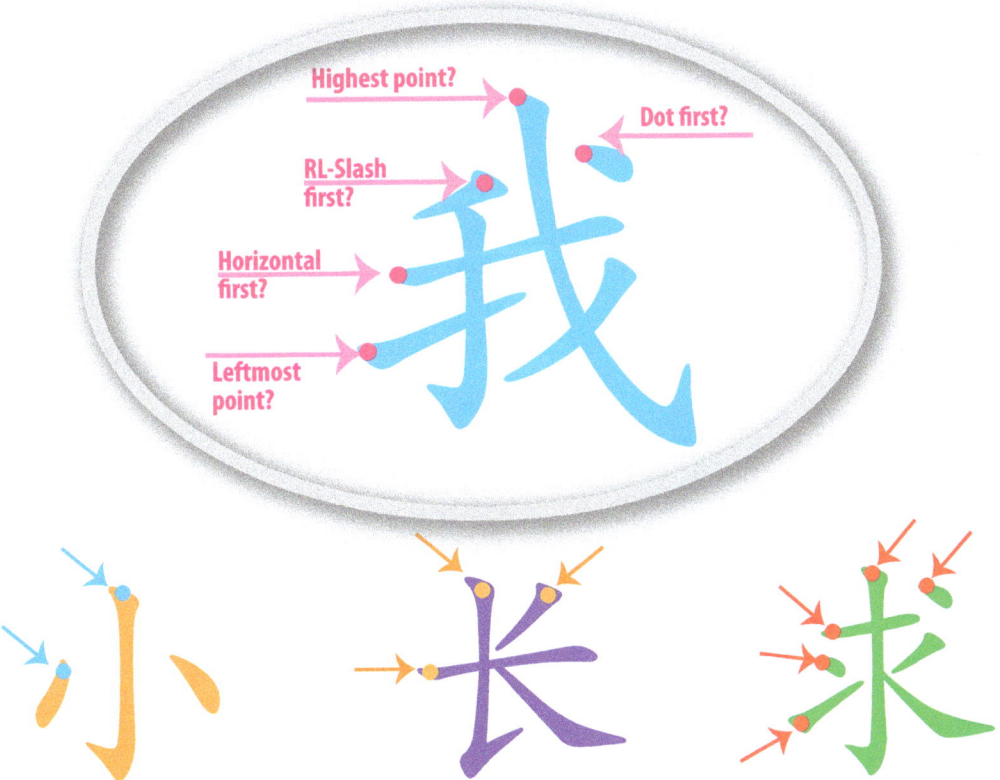

WHAT YOU'LL LEARN

① *Part Order & Structure of Chinese Characters*

Characters that follow Standard Part Order Rules

Characters with Intersecting Parts

Characters with Unique Part Order

② *Application of Part Order Rules*

Write Chinese characters in correct part order

Form complex characters using simple structures

Differentiate between similar-looking characters

Target audiences

This series of books will benefit learners whose key language is English or languages with words formed in only left-to-right combination.

CONTENT

List of Activities

SCOPE
REDEFINING THE COMPOSITION OF CHINESE CHARACTERS

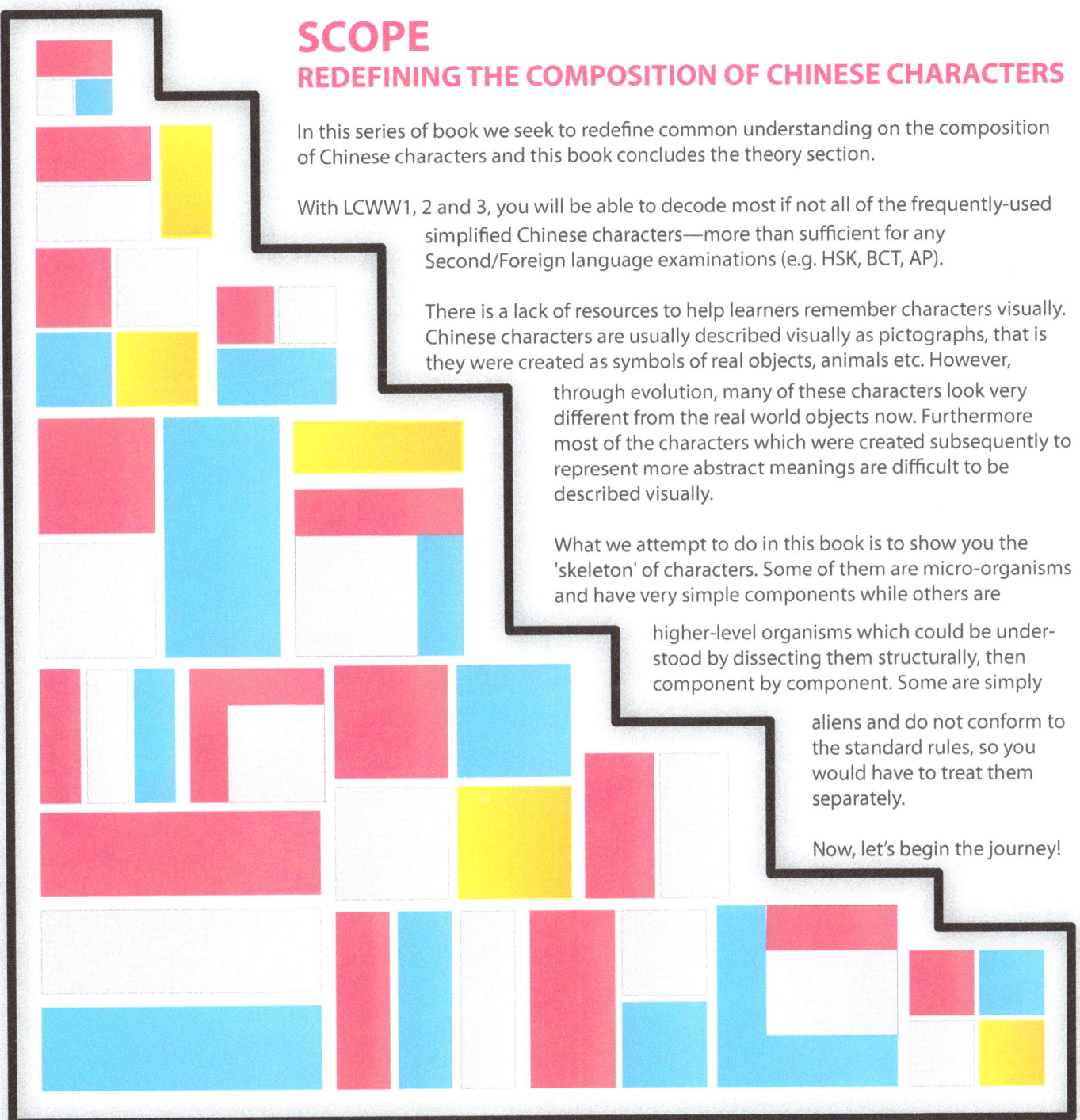

In this series of book we seek to redefine common understanding on the composition of Chinese characters and this book concludes the theory section.

With LCWW1, 2 and 3, you will be able to decode most if not all of the frequently-used simplified Chinese characters—more than sufficient for any Second/Foreign language examinations (e.g. HSK, BCT, AP).

There is a lack of resources to help learners remember characters visually. Chinese characters are usually described visually as pictographs, that is they were created as symbols of real objects, animals etc. However, through evolution, many of these characters look very different from the real world objects now. Furthermore most of the characters which were created subsequently to represent more abstract meanings are difficult to be described visually.

What we attempt to do in this book is to show you the 'skeleton' of characters. Some of them are micro-organisms and have very simple components while others are higher-level organisms which could be understood by dissecting them structurally, then component by component. Some are simply aliens and do not conform to the standard rules, so you would have to treat them separately.

Now, let's begin the journey!

Introduction

Redefine Composition

Line versus Square

Starting Point

Inadequate Stroke Order Guidelines

How You'll Learn

Write In Your Mind

Recaps

Learning English on

PLANET Q

Imagine you are going to visit Planet Q, a faraway planet. To communicate with the residents there, you have to learn their language. They also speak English but their English is different from English on Planet Earth. Find out more ...

English on Planet Q
240 Alphabets

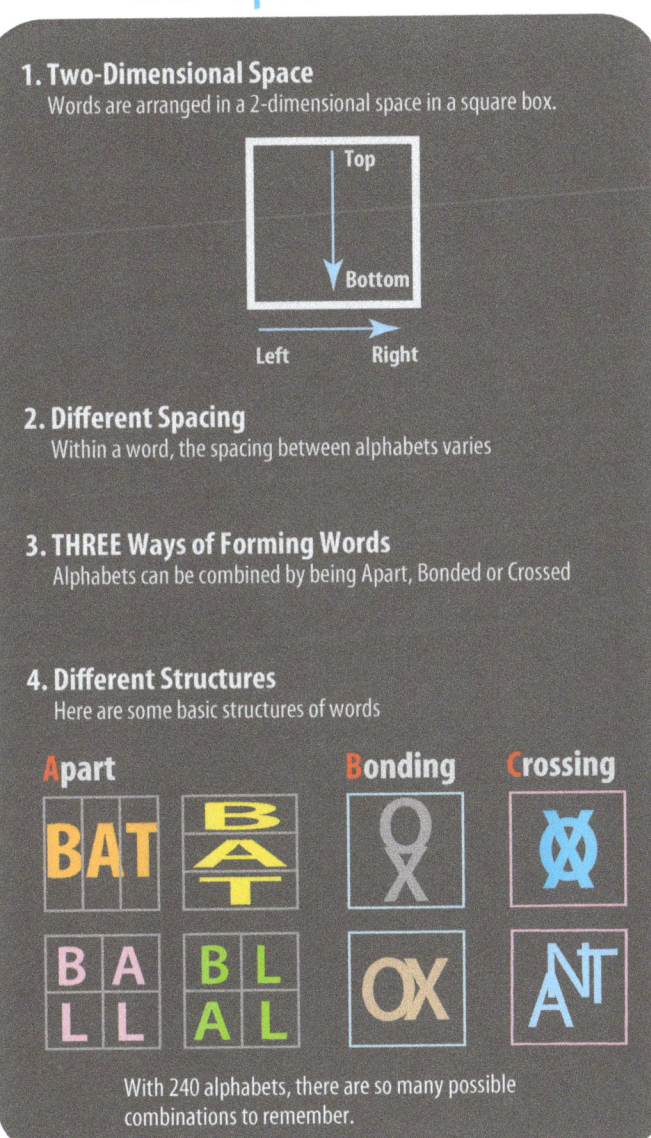

1. Two-Dimensional Space
Words are arranged in a 2-dimensional space in a square box.

Top
Bottom
Left   Right

2. Different Spacing
Within a word, the spacing between alphabets varies

3. THREE Ways of Forming Words
Alphabets can be combined by being Apart, Bonded or Crossed

4. Different Structures
Here are some basic structures of words

Apart   Bonding   Crossing

BAT   BAT   OX   OX
BALL   LAL   OX   ANT

With 240 alphabets, there are so many possible combinations to remember.

English on Planet Earth
26 Alphabets

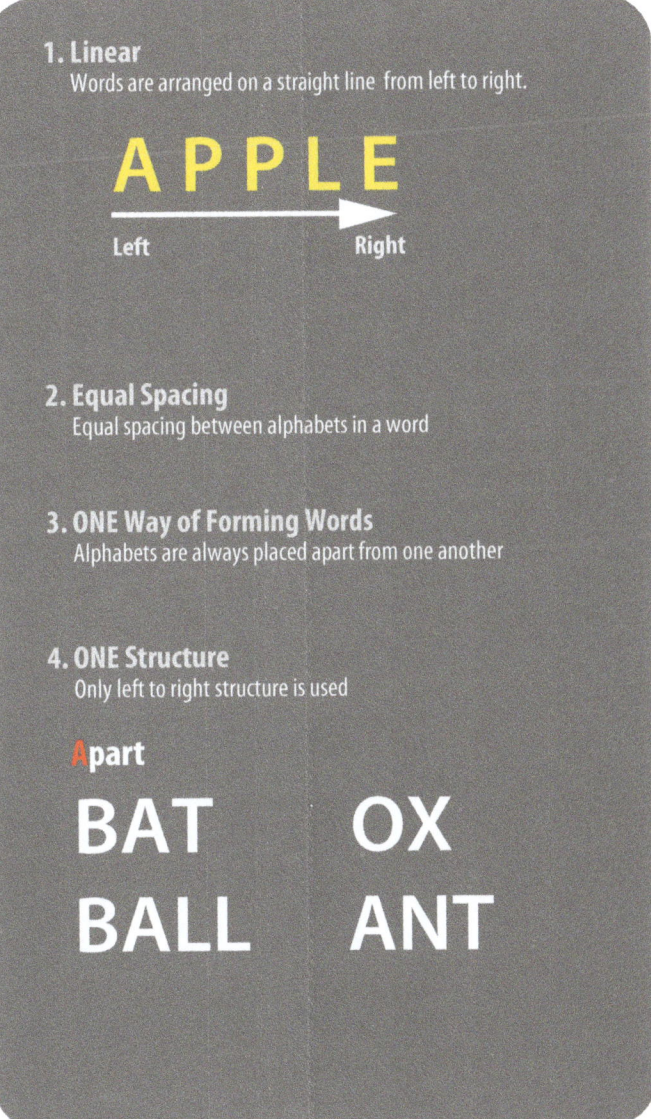

1. Linear
Words are arranged on a straight line from left to right.

APPLE
Left   Right

2. Equal Spacing
Equal spacing between alphabets in a word

3. ONE Way of Forming Words
Alphabets are always placed apart from one another

4. ONE Structure
Only left to right structure is used

Apart

BAT   OX
BALL   ANT

English on Planet Q

Learning English on Planet Q is more difficult because you will

1. **NOT be taught the 240 alphabets**
   before learning the words, which means you have to figure out the alphabets on your own as you learn the words!

2. **NOT be taught how to 'spell' the alphabets**
   to form words in a systematic way Again, you have to figure out the structures of words on your own as you learn the words!

3. **NOT taught the order the alphabets**
   as the alphabets are not arranged in a fixed order.

English on Planet Earth

On Planet Earth, by comparison, English is so much easier to learn because you

1. **Learn the 26 alphabets**
   before learning English words so you know any word can be formed by just 26 alphabets. It is manageable and easy to grasp.

2. **Learn that there is only ONE way to 'spell'**
   the alphabets, that is from left to right on a straight line.

3. **Learn the 26 alphabets arranged in a fixed order**
   from A to Z so it is easy to recall the alphabets.

Chinese language on Planet Earth shares all the features of English on Planet Q. Now, you understand better why Chinese characters are so difficult to remember if they are not taught systemtically. In LCWW2, we resolved problems 1 and 3 mentiioned above (alphabets and order of alphabets) and now in this book, we are going to provide the solution for problem 2 (spell the words).

STARTING POINT

Check your answers for this activity.

Did you get the answers correct?

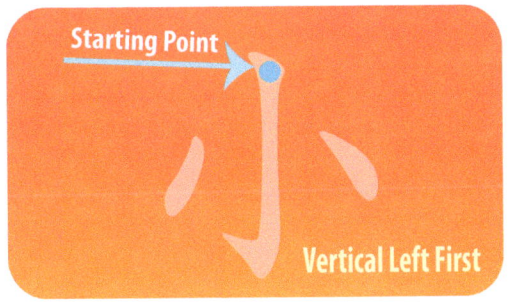

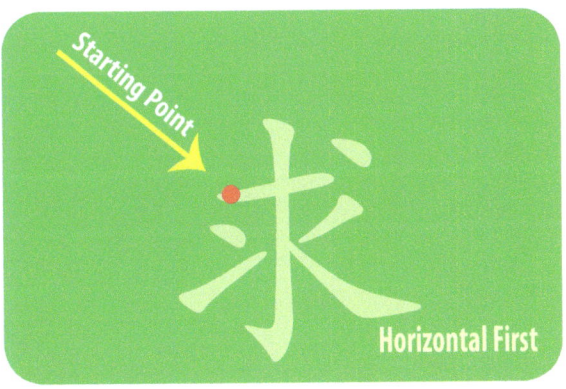

Are you able to identify
any guiding principle(s)
to help you remember
the starting point of the characters?

You will realise that the general guideline that the starting point usually starts from the shaded grids within the square box *(see page vii)* may not help much as there could be more than one stroke starting in these grids for these characters.

Looking out for the leftmost or topmost point in a character is also not a good indication on the starting point of a character. Sometimes, the starting point may not be any of the extreme points (outermost points) of a character.

In conclusion, the current ways of identifying the starting point of a character do not provide sufficient guidelines for beginners.

See next page for another reason...

WHY STROKE ORDER GUIDELINES ARE INADEQUATE?

As mentioned on page *v*, the currrent stroke order guidelines given in some textbooks do not provide sufficient guidance to cover the few thousands Chinese characters. Here are some of the reasons:

1. It is difficult to apply the rules if
   a) Characters have many bonded and crossed strokes:

   我 裁 栽 成 臧

   b) Characters do not follow the common structures:

   凹 凸 爽 渊 鼎

3. The guidelines are shown in text with some examples and not presented visually.

4. For some characters, the rules are contradictory. See exceptions below.

This series of books seek to fill the learning gap. Upon completion of this book, you will be able to remember these characters easily.

Exceptions to the Stroke Order Guidelines

1. Horizontal(s) before Vertical

Examples

Exceptions

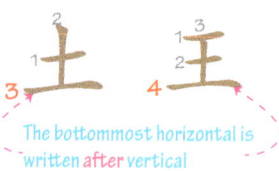

The bottommost horizontal is written after vertical

2. Left to Right

Example

Exception

The middle dots are written after the strokes on the sides

3. Middle before Sides

Example

Exception

The middle strokes are written after the sides (dots).

4. Outside, Inside then Close (enclosure)

Example

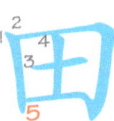

Exception

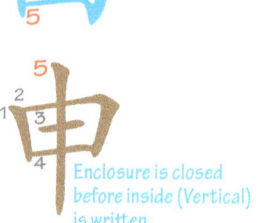

Enclosure is closed before inside (Vertical) is written

5. Outside before Inside for characters enclosed on the top and right sides

Example

Exception

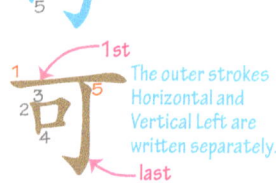

1st

The outer strokes Horizontal and Vertical Left are written separately.

last

6. Inside before Outside for characters enclosed on the bottom and left sides

Example

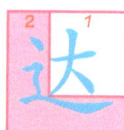

Exception

Outside (bottom and left sides) are written first

HOW YOU'LL LEARN

You will learn Chinese characters systematically according to their appearance—from simple structure to more complex ones —starting from single stroke to single alphabet to Standard Part Order to Unique Part Order. Characters with more complex structures can be decoded using these simpler structures.

1. SIMPLE RULES

are rules of thumb to help you learn quickly and efficiently.

(A) STROKE ORDER RULES

qTRAILS Alphabets can be remembered easily through the **32 stroke patterns** taught in LCWW2.

(B) PART ORDER RULES

Characters with multiple parts can be remembered via the Standard Part Order Rules, Unique Part Order Rules and Part Order of Intersecting Parts

2. SYMBOLS

PART ORDER SYMBOLS

Symbols associated with these part order rules are presented together to help you visualise the structures.

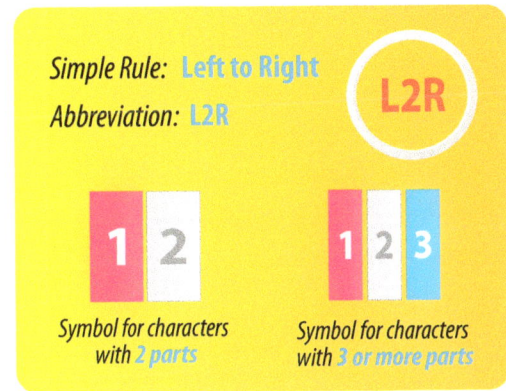

Simple Rule: **Left to Right**

Abbreviation: **L2R**

L2R

Symbol for characters with *2 parts*

Symbol for characters with *3 or more parts*

3. COLOURS

To help you to learn visually, we introduce another set of 6-colour code for the Part Order of characters. These colours are also used in the symbols. You will be able to see how characters can be put together in a certain order in the square box easily. In contrast to Chinese characters in black, you will be able to distinguish these colour-coded characters easily.

Remember the 6 colours—*pink, white, light blue, yellow, purple and green*.

6-Colour Code (Part Order)

Part Order
1 2 3 4 5 6

4. BOND POINT & CROSS POINT OF PARTS

In LCWW2, we analysed the relationships between strokes in alphabets—whether they are apart, bonded or crossed. In this book, we will analyse the relationships between **PARTS—qTRAIL Alphabets** and **35 strokes**.

Instead of finding the Bond Point (BP) and Cross Point (CP) of strokes, we will look at **BP and CP of parts**. Note the symbols used are slightly different from those shown in previous books.

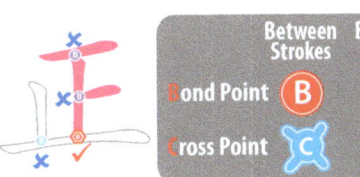

	Between Strokes	Between Parts
Bond Point	B	B
Cross Point	C	C

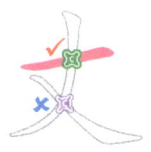

'WRITE' IN YOUR MIND

In LCWW2, we discussed **whether it is necessary to write the strokes in Chinese characters in a fixed order**. Writing them in a particular order helps you to remember and compare the characters and their parts better.

In LCWW1, we also discussed **if it is necessary to write characters by hand** to develop your muscle memory. Our recommendation then was to write minimally and purposefully but not too much that it becomes overbearing and resulted in you losing interest.

By now, you will realise that you can achieve the same and even better results by learning to see visually. This method is a good alternative to learners who are unable or dislike to write. We believe that learning to 'SEE' is the first priority.

In this book, we are introducing the concept '**Write in your mind**'. When you see a character, don't see it as a stack of sticks piling on top of one another. Instead see the character to be composed of distinctive and recognisable alphabets and/or strokes appearing in sequence. Visualise the alphabets/strokes in colours, see them appearing one by one according to the sequence. Note if there are any bond points or cross points.

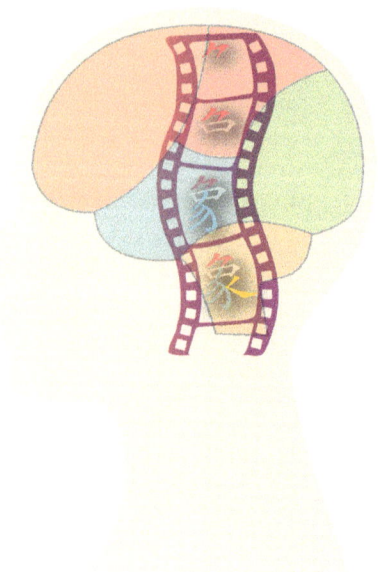

RECAPS

To help you revise what you have learnt in LCWW1 and LCWW2, the next few pages cover the 35 strokes (LCWW1) and the basic qTRAILS Alphabets (LCWW2).

Names of Strokes (Page 9)
The names of the 35 basic strokes used to form alphabets and Chinese characters are shown in the next page. **What-You-See-Is-What-You-Name** (WYSIWYN), that is the strokes are named according their appearance, so it is easy to remember the names. Return to the page if you come across any stroke name that you cannot remember.

qTRAILS Alphabets (Basic) (Page 10 - 11)
In this activity, only the basic qTRAILS Alphabets of the 32 qTRAILS are covered. They represent the 32 stroke patterns. After you have learnt the basic alphabets, it will be easy to extend the knowledge to **variations** and **exceptions** of these basic alphabets.

35 Strokes

In this book, characters are presented in PARTS (strokes and qTRAILS alphabets). Now, let us revise the 35 strokes. More activities on these strokes in LCWW1.

1. Vertical
2. Vertical Left
3. Vertical Right
4. Horizontal
5. Horizontal Hook
6. RL-Slash
7. LR-Slash
8. Hunchback
9. Leanback
10. Curl-Up
11. RL-Dot
12. LR-Dot
13. Tick
14. 7-Bend
15. 7-Hook
16. 7-Leanback
17. Acute-7
18. 7-Back-kick
19. 7-Slash
20. L-Bend
21. Round-L
22. L-Hook
23. Boomerang
24. Acute-L
25. L7-Bends
26. L7-Hook
27. Lightning
28. 7L-Bends
29. Round-7L
30. 7L-Hook
31. Z-Hook
32. Double-7 Bends
33. Double-7 Hook
34. Double-7 Slash
35. Acute-7 Hunchback

Learn Chinese without WRITING

qTRAILS™ Alphabets
(32 Stroke Patterns)

Cut out the alphabets on page 231 and paste them into the correct qTRAILS to form the basic qTRAILS Map. Observe the stroke order of the alphabets to find out how the alphabets fit in.

1 三 川 彡 ☐

2 ⟍ ⟀ ⟋ ⟍

3 ⟍ ⟨ ⟍

4 凵 夕 マ

5 ⼨ ⼰ ⼹

6 ☐ ⼃ ⼱ ☐ ⼌

7 牛 ☐ 巾 中

8 十 干 ⼲ ☐ ⼲ 手

9 廾 ☐ 卅 ☐ 井

10 大 天 夫 ☐ 夫

11 木 未 ☐ 末

12 土 王 ☐ 丰 ☐ 丰

13 八 人 ☐ 之 辶

14 亻 ☐ 亻 ⼈

15 ⟨ ⟍

16 乂 ☐ 又 子

© 2016 W.Q. BLOSH. All rights reserved.

qTRAILS™ Alphabets
(32 Stroke Patterns)

Stroke Order
1 2 3 4 5 6

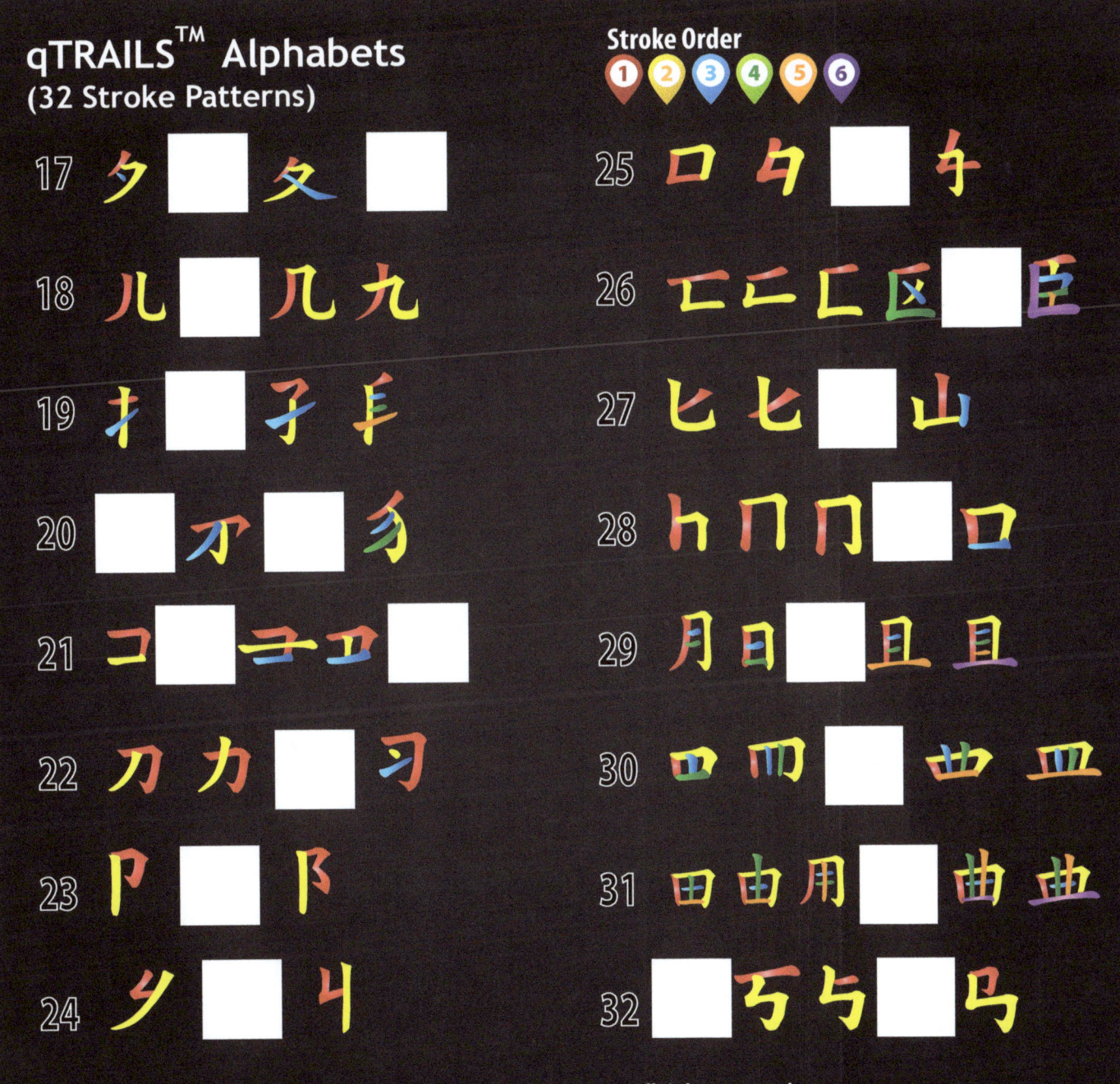

17　夕　☐　夂　☐

18　儿　☐　几　九

19　才　☐　子　手

20　☐　才　☐　彡

21　コ　☐　子　卫　☐

22　刀　力　☐　习

23　卩　☐　阝

24　夕　☐　屮

25　口　夕　☐　キ

26　匸　匸　匚　区　☐　臣

27　匕　七　☐　山

28　九　几　几　☐　口

29　月　日　☐　且　且

30　甲　皿　☐　曲　皿

31　田　由　用　☐　曲　曲

32　☐　丂　与　☐　马

Check your answers on pages 206 - 209

STORY I: COLOURFUL PERFORMERS

The Story

To many people, strokes are like tadpoles

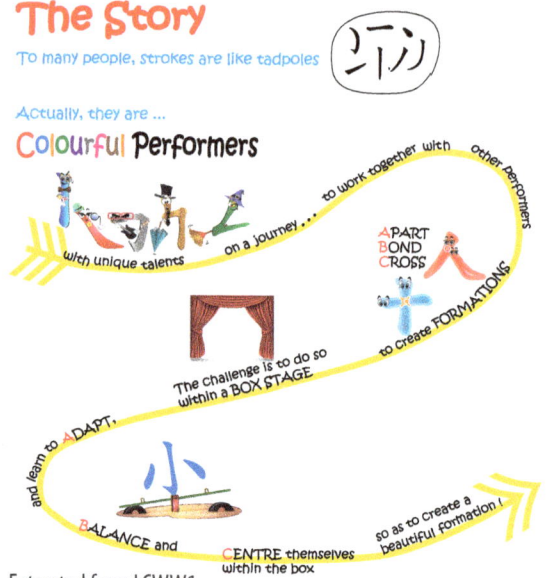

Extracted from LCWW1

STORY II: GOING TO BOOT CAMPS

Extracted from LCWW2

STORY III: ACTUAL PERFORMANCES

After the performers graduated from the Boot Camps where they learnt how to create partial formations (alphabets) according to the 32 stroke patterns, they are now ready to perform.

In actual performances, they will create the full formations (characters) quickly in the square box. See the next page.

Terms Used in the Story

* Strokes = Performers

* Chinese Alphabets = Partial Formations

* Characters = Formations

5 Strokes

Remember we mentioned that 5 performers did not participate in the boot camps. They will be going straight to the performances. In other words, these performers (strokes) do not appear in partial formations (alphabets), they will turn up in the full formations (characters).

Z-Hook: 乙 乞

L7-Bends: 鼎

7L-Bends: 凹

Double-7 Bends: 凸

Curl-Up: 心 必

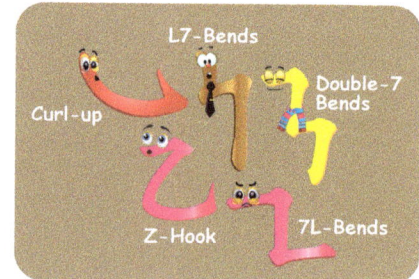

The Story III ...

Playing Lego

Previously ...
in the boot camps, the Performers (strokes)
learnt to create Chinese APLHABETS
(Partial Formations)

Now ...
they are ready to
perform

They will combine the Parts
(alphabets or strokes) to create
CHARACTERS (Full Formations)

It is fun ...
it is like playing the
Lego game

WHAT YOU NEED TO DO

To help you remember the Part Order Rules better, interact with the book these ways:

1 **(1) Read the rule** *(e.g. Left to Right)* L2R *Simple Rule:* **Left to Right**

2 **(2) Visualise the Part Order** *through the symbol, colours and numberings*

3 **(3) Distinguish and colour the parts** *according to the Part Order Colour Code*

4 **(4) Write in your mind** *Say 'pink', visualise first part ...)*

5 (5) Review

6 **(4) Construct and deconstruct characters**

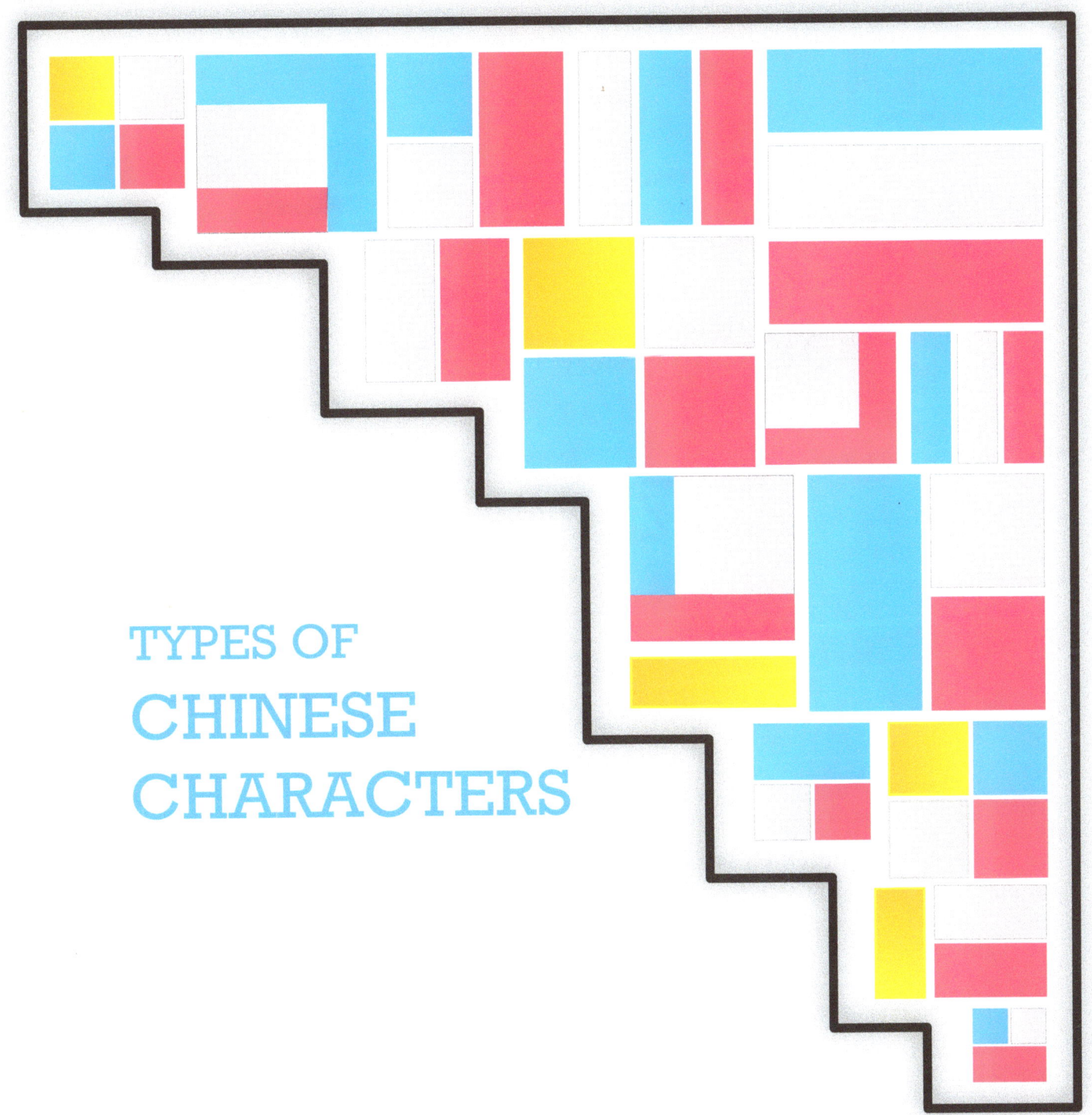

TYPES OF CHINESE CHARACTERS

LCWW1:

35

STROKES

6 STROKE ORDER
COLOURS

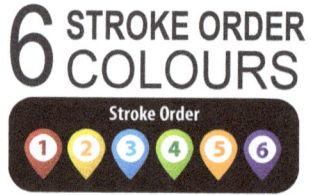

LCWW2:

32 STROKE ORDER
PATTERNS

240 qTRAILS
ALPHABETS

LCWW3:

7 PART ORDER
RULES

6 PART ORDER
COLOURS

TYPES OF CHINESE CHARACTERS

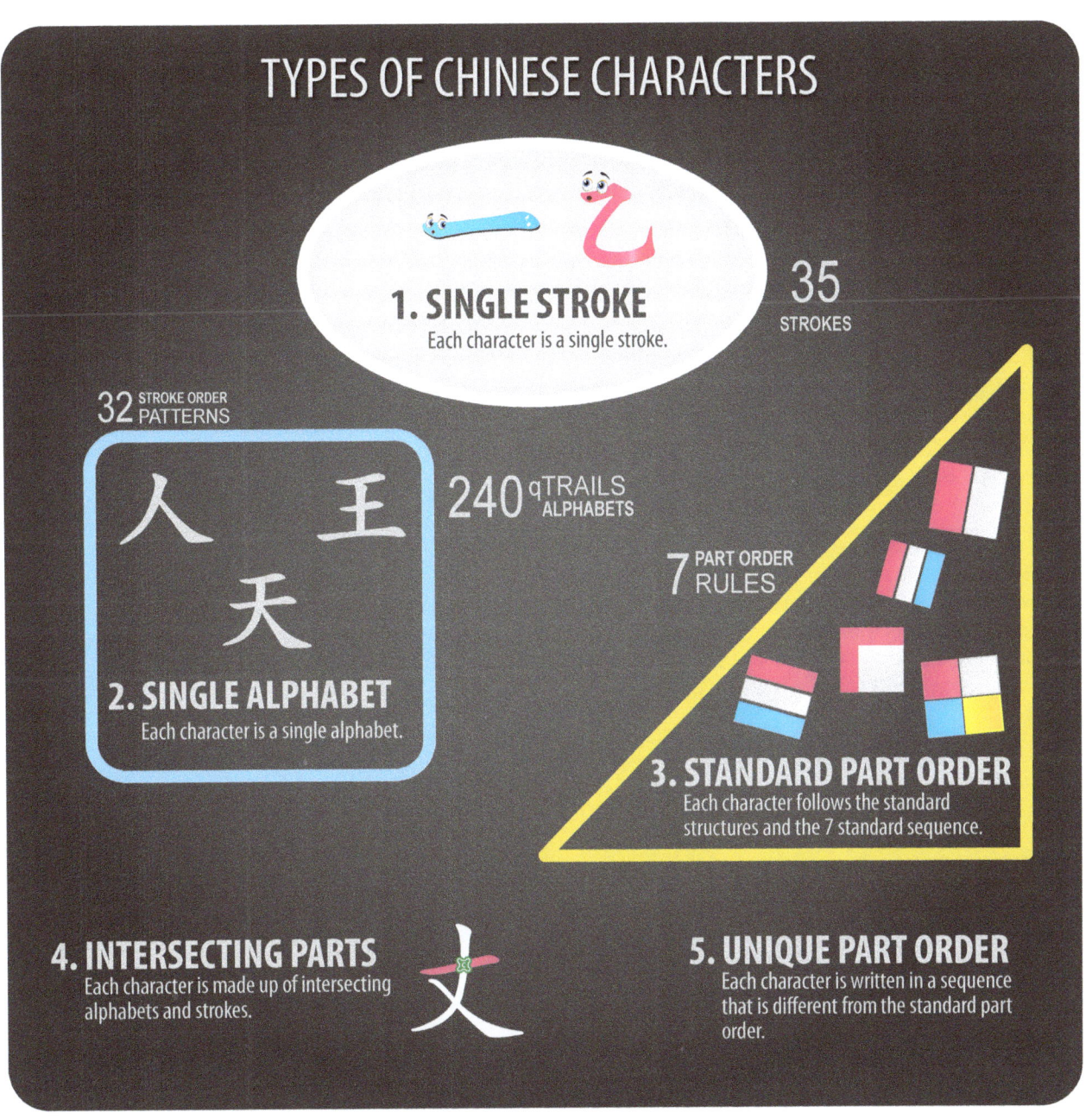

1. SINGLE STROKE
Each character is a single stroke.

35 STROKES

32 STROKE ORDER PATTERNS

240 qTRAILS ALPHABETS

2. SINGLE ALPHABET
Each character is a single alphabet.

7 PART ORDER RULES

3. STANDARD PART ORDER
Each character follows the standard structures and the 7 standard sequence.

4. INTERSECTING PARTS
Each character is made up of intersecting alphabets and strokes.

5. UNIQUE PART ORDER
Each character is written in a sequence that is different from the standard part order.

HOW CHARACTERS ARE FORMED

Characters from LCWW1 and 2

In LCWW1 you learnt **35 strokes**, only two (一、乙) of these single strokes are characters. In LCWW2, you learnt **240 qTRAILS Alphabets** organised according to the 32 Stroke Patterns. Some of these alphabets are also characters themselves which means they are meaningful and can be used to form vocabularies. Do the revision activities on pages 21-23 to find out which qTRAILS these characters belong to.

Characters from LCWW3

In LCWW3, you will learn more characters formed according to the **7 Part Order Rules (7POR)**, the standard part order that can be used to form most of the Chinese characters. There are some exceptions that have **Intersecting Parts** or **Unique Part Order (UPO)**.

7 Part Order Rules (Type 3)

Most characters follow the standard structures in their formations and can be summarised into 7 Part Order Rules (7POR). The components in these characters are **Apart** or **Bonded** to one another. A minority of these characters have parts that **Crossed** one another. *(recall the 'Triple ABCs Concept' in LCWW1)*.

Part Order of Intersecting Parts (Type 4)

Characters with parts that are **Crossed** (i.e. overlapping one another) may confuse some beginners as the strokes look tangled. Some common patterns are observable. These characters are presented systematically to help you see patterns within them and separate the parts at one glance.

Unique Part Order (Type 5)

Characters with unique part sequence violate the standard rules and have to be remembered individually. These are rare and few.

Simple to Complex (Type 6)

What about characters with complex structures?

These characters can be formed by characters with simpler structures. They will look easy to you as you will be able to identify patterns within them using the knowledge you learnt in LCWW1, 2 and 3.

Differences between Types 2 and 3 Characters

Type 2 (Single Alphabets)

* *Has 2 to 6 strokes*

* *Made up of single strokes*

* *Are formed according to the 32 Stroke Patterns*

Type 3 (Standard Part Order)

* *Has 6 or more strokes*

* *Made up of alphabets (A) and strokes (S):*

  A+S or **A+A**

* *Are formed by using standard structures*

Differences between Types 3 and 4 Characters

Type 3 (Standard Part Order)

* *Have parts (alphabets and strokes) that are placed **Apart** from one another or **Bonded** to one another or **Crossed** one another.*

Type 4 (Intersecting Parts)

* *Have parts (alphabets and strokes) that **Crossed** one another.*

Characters from LCWW1 & 2

Single Stroke

Single qTRAILS **Alphabet**

Introducing Horizontal and Z-Hook

Remember in LCWW2, Z-Hook did not attend the boot camps.

Horizontal

B

Z-Hook

B

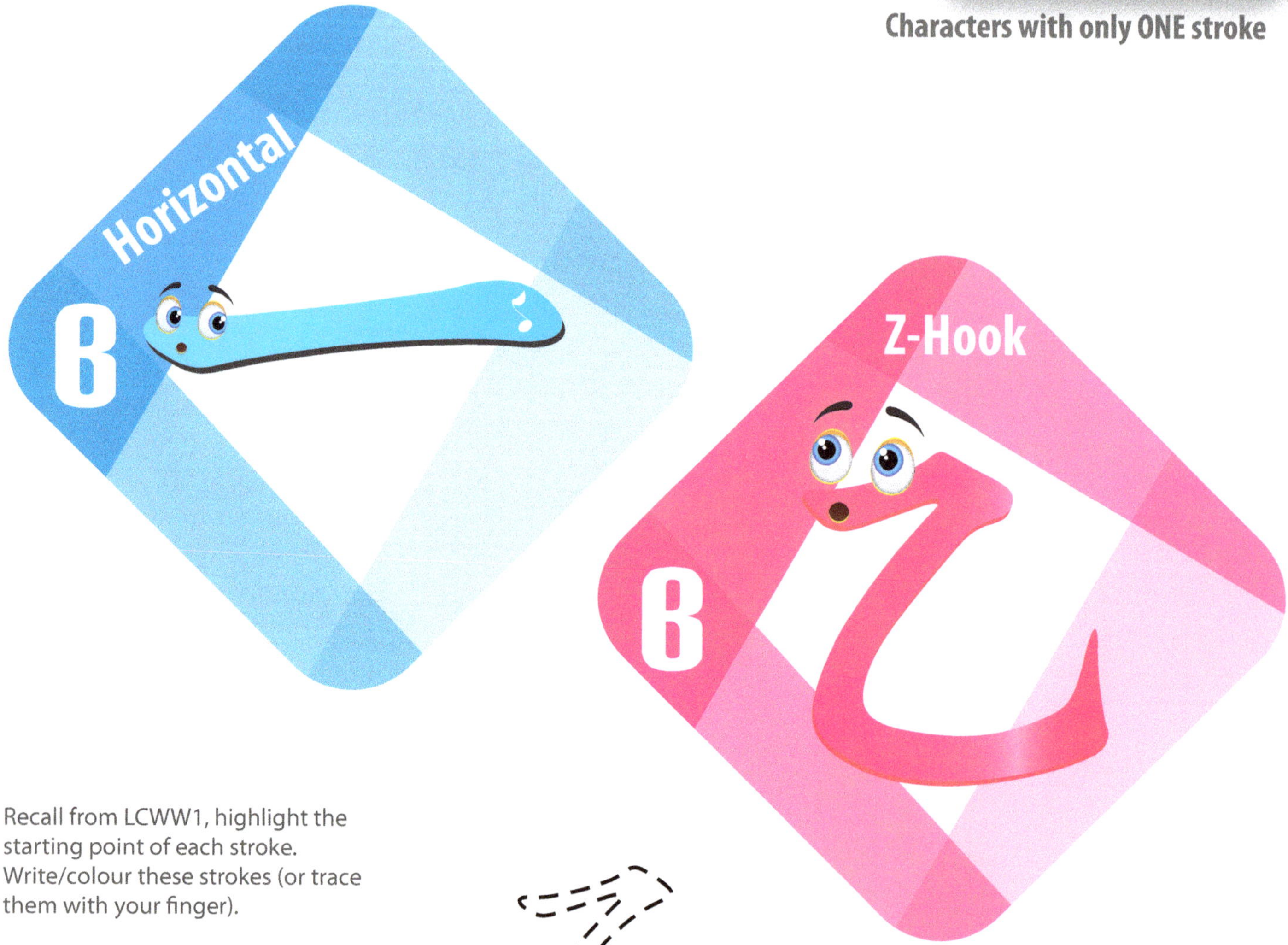

Recall from LCWW1, highlight the starting point of each stroke. Write/colour these strokes (or trace them with your finger).

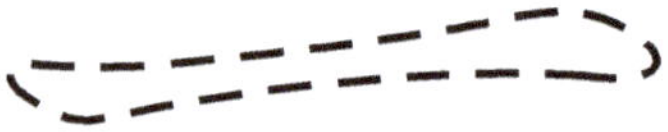

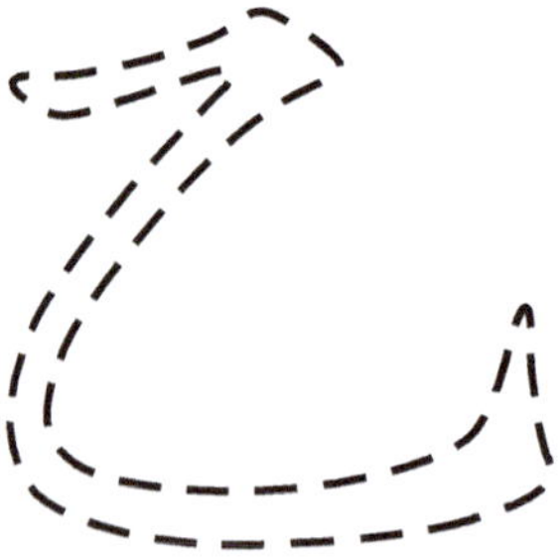

Activity 1

Alphabets are parts within characters, some are also characters, that is they have meanings and can be used to form vocabularies. Link up the alphabets from the same qTRAIL. Note that variations of the basic qTRAILS are also included in this activity. (*Variations* share the same stroke order as basic alphabets)

Activity 2

These alphabets are also characters. Mix and match each row of alphabets to the names of the qTRAILS.

1.

2.

3.

4.

5.

6.

7.

8.

9.

- a) **Split** (Simple)

- b) **Split & Cross** (L-Hook / 7L-Hook)

- c) **Marching**

- d) **Tick**

- e) **Perpendiculars** (T-Shape)

- f) **Final Dot**

- g) **Cross** (7-Slash)

- h) **Perpendiculars** (Half Ladder)

- i) **Cross** (Simple)

Activity 3

These alphabets are also characters. Mix and match each row of alphabets to the names of the qTRAILS.

Single Alphabet

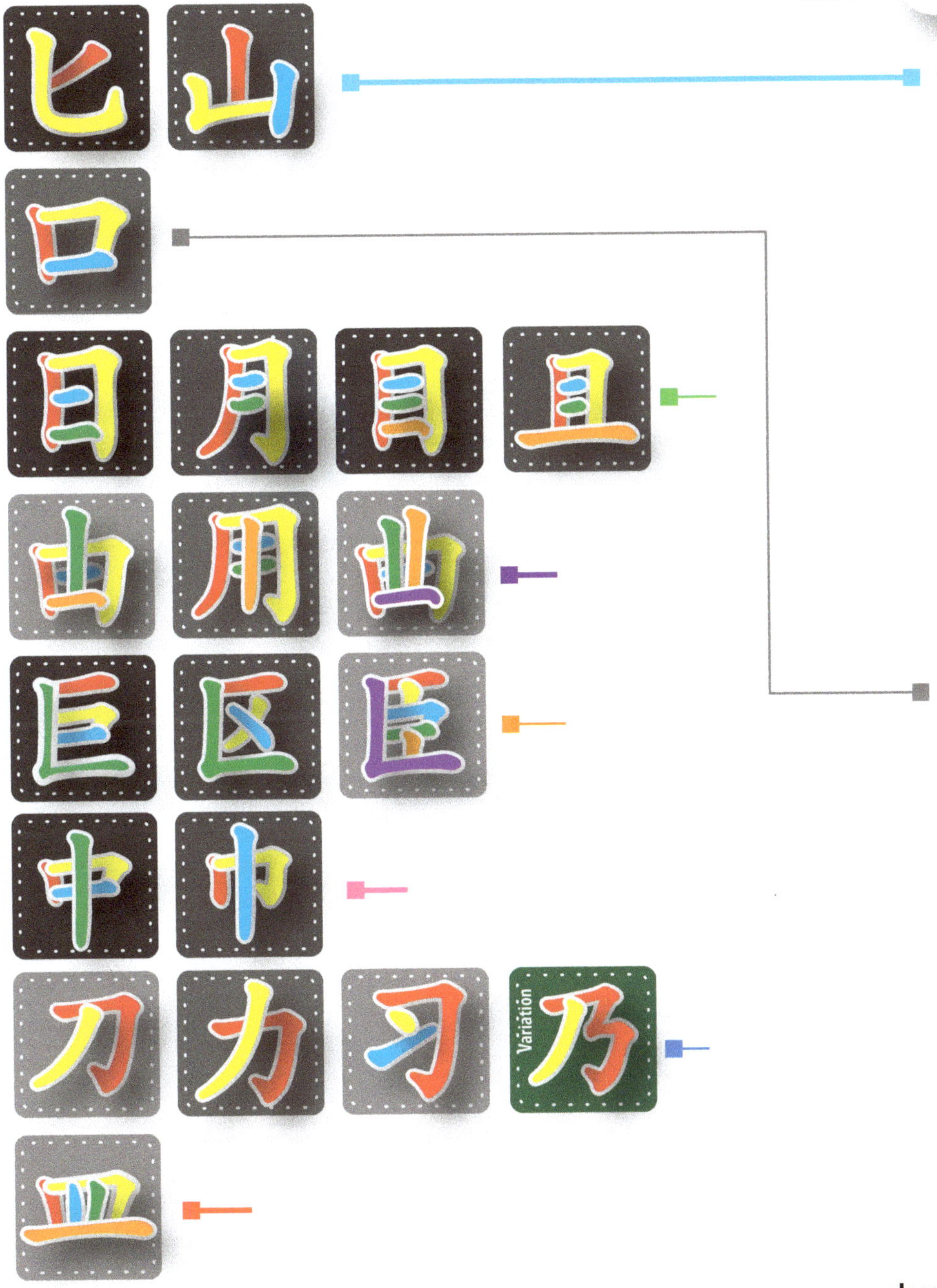

a) **L-Frame & U-Frame**

b) **Skewer**

c) **Enclosure** (Vertical)

d) **7-Hook Frame**

e) **n-Frame / Enclosure** (Empty)

f) **C-Frame**

g) **Enclosure** (Horizontal)

h) **Enclosure** (Intersections)

RECAP: Triple ABCs Concepts

3rd Set of ABC (ABC3)
UNSPOKEN RULES OF CHINESE CHARACTERS

Adapt

Size Adaptation
How a part in a character changes its dimensions *(slim downs, flattens or shrinks)* to fit into the character.

Stroke Adaptation
How a stroke of a part changes *(stretches, shortens, changes angle to horizontal, transforms)* itself to fit into another character.

Balance

Balance
How symmetrical, mostly symmetrical or non-symmetrical characters appear stable and aesthetically pleasing.

Centre

Centre
How parts within a character are spaced out and positioned, usually in relation to the centre of the character so that the character looks balanced.

Triple ABCs Concept consists of three sets of ABC:
1. Angles, Bends, Curves
2. Apart, Bonding, Crossing
3. Adapt, Balance, Centre

The first set of ABC explains the characteristics of strokes; the second set is on how the strokes combine with one another to create characters and the last set reveals the aesthetic requirements of characters. The first and second sets of ABCs were discussed in LCWW1 and 2.

STANDARD
PART ORDER

The characters (alphabets) introduced so far are mostly from LCWW2, only two characters (single stroke) from LCWW1. The stroke order of these characters are presented using the Stroke Order Colour Code.

In LCWW3, characters, made up of alphabets and strokes, will be introduced using the Part Order Colour Code. Now, try to recall the sequence of this set of colours.

Activity 4

Number the sequence of the colours for the **Parts Order.**

01 T2B — Top to Bottom

L2R — Left to Right

Combi — Combinations of T2B and L2R

02

03 M4S — Middle before Sides

S4M — Sides before Middle

04 O4I — Outside before Inside

I4O — Inside before Outside

05 OIO — Outside-Inside-Outside

06 FPF — Flag Pole First

FPL — Flag Pole Last

07 DOF — Dot(s) First

DOL — Dot(s) Last

7 PART ORDER RULES

Learn Chinese *without* WRITING 3

Prepare this book to be the reference which you can use to refer to the stroke sequence of character

Show accurate colour representations so that you can see at a glance

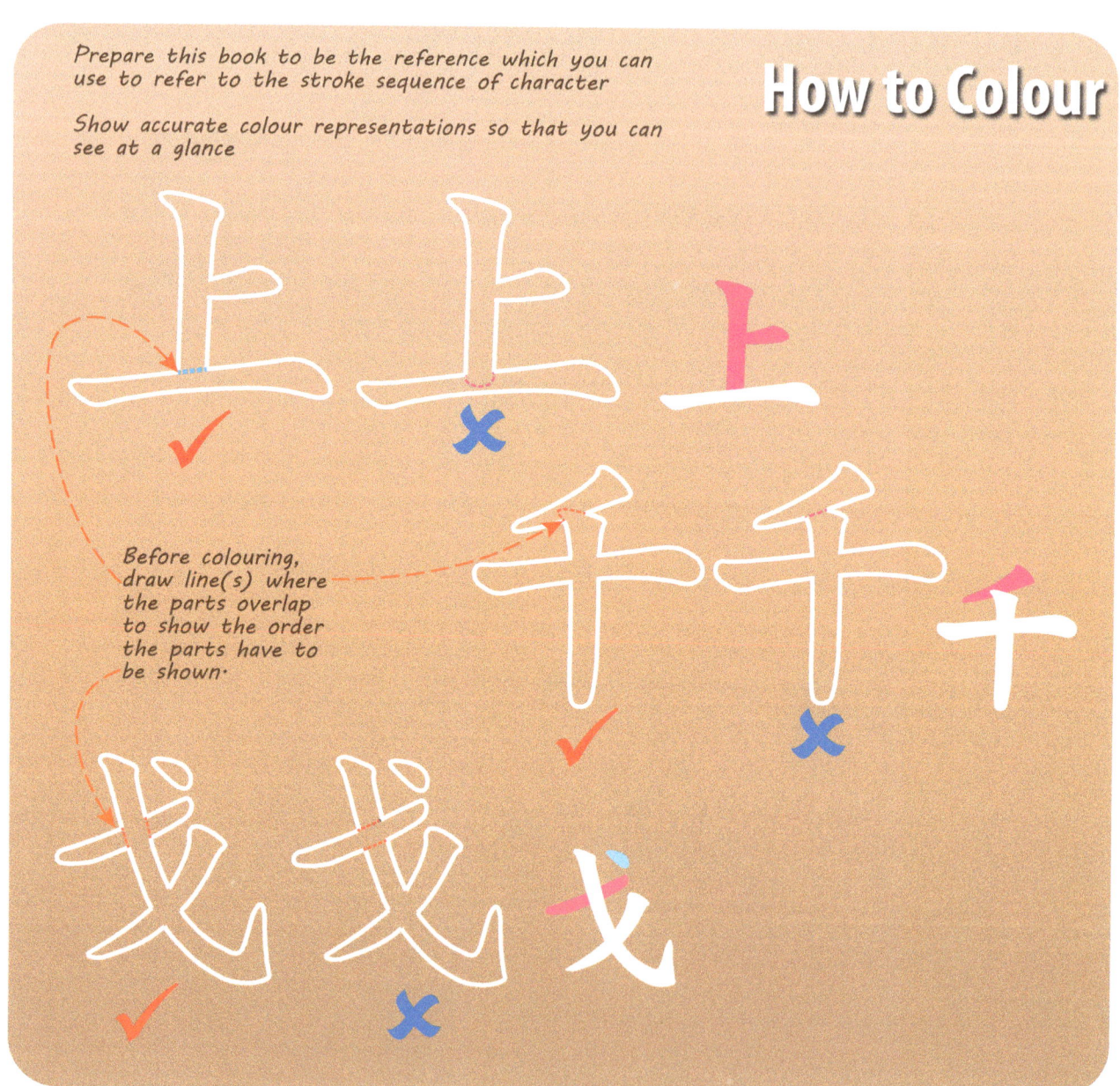

Before colouring, draw line(s) where the parts overlap to show the order the parts have to be shown.

01

T2B
Top to Bottom

L2R
Left to Right

(A) Alphabet + Stroke(s)

(B) Alphabet + Alphabet

(C) Alphabet(s) + Stroke(s)

(A) Alphabet + *Strokes*

1. *Horizontal*
2. *Vertical*
3. *RL-Slash*
4. *L-Hook*
5. *L7-Hook*

Part Order: TOP DOWN

These characters are created by placing a horizontal and a qTRAIL alphabet **A**part or **B**onding them together.

Part Order

Colour according to the order of the parts

BP within alphabet will NOT be shown

Part Order: LEFT RIGHT

Bonding a RL-Slash and a qTRAIL alphabet from left to right creates this character:

Enclosure (Horizontal) *[qTRAILS 29]*

Apart

State the qTRAIL this alphabet belongs

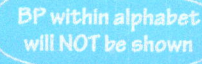

Perpendicular (Half Ladder) *[qTRAILS 5]*

Bonding

Bond Point (BP) of the two parts

Intersections (Split) *[qTRAILS 10]*

Bonding

Characters with strokes **C**rossing one another are more difficult to distinguish and will be introduced in another section.

Activity 5

Colour these two-part characters (**horizontal and qTRAIL alphabet**) according to the colours given, moving from **top down**. The qTRAIL alphabet in each character is identified. Look up the qTRAILS in the qTRAILS Map if you are unsure.

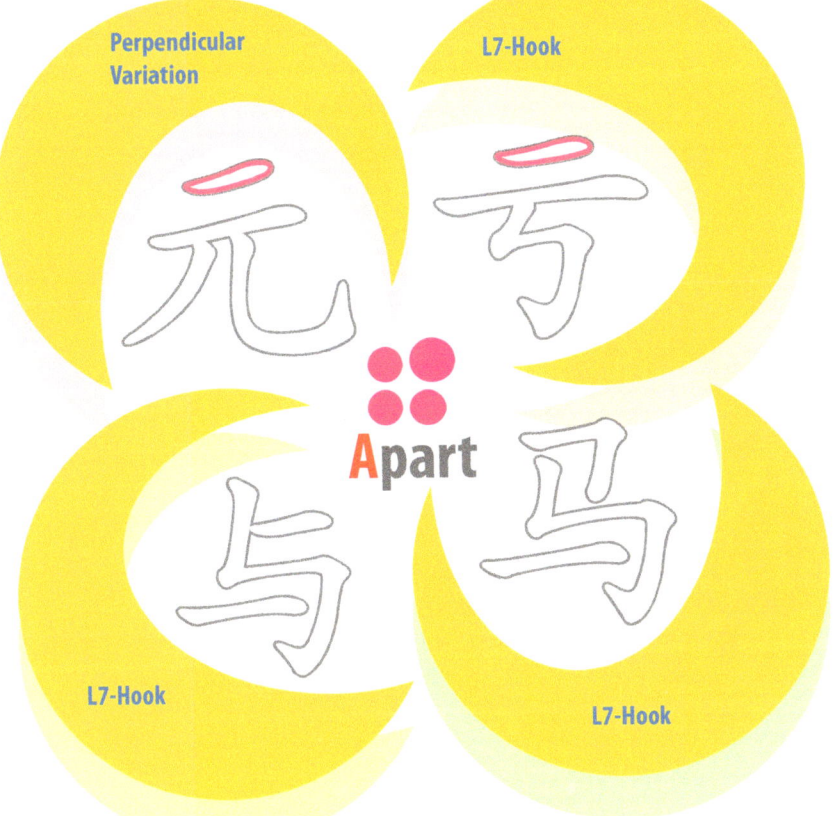

Perpendicular Variation

L7-Hook

L7-Hook

L7-Hook

Apart

Part Order
1 2

In these two characters, the Bond Point (BP) is shown.

Bonding

Split (7-Slash)

Flag (7-Hook)

Activity 6

Colour these two-part characters (**vertical and qTRAIL alphabet**) according to the colours given, moving from **top down** or from **left to right**. The qTRAIL alphabet is named in each character. Look up the qTRAILS if you are unsure.

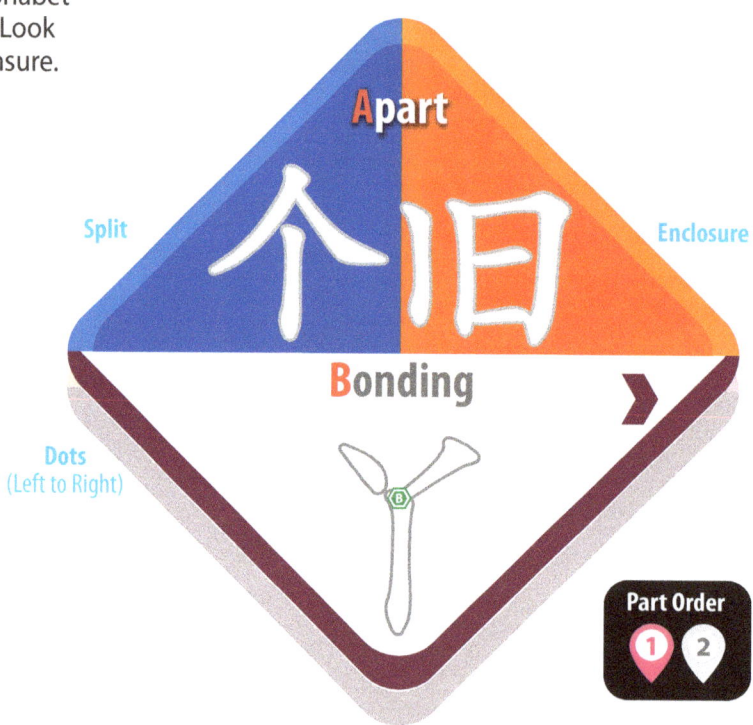

 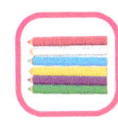

Activity 7

Colour these two-part characters (**RL-Slash and qTRAIL alphabet**) according to the colours given, moving from **top down** or from **left to right**. The qTRAIL alphabet is named in each character. Look up the qTRAILS if you are unsure. Bond points for some of the characters are shown.

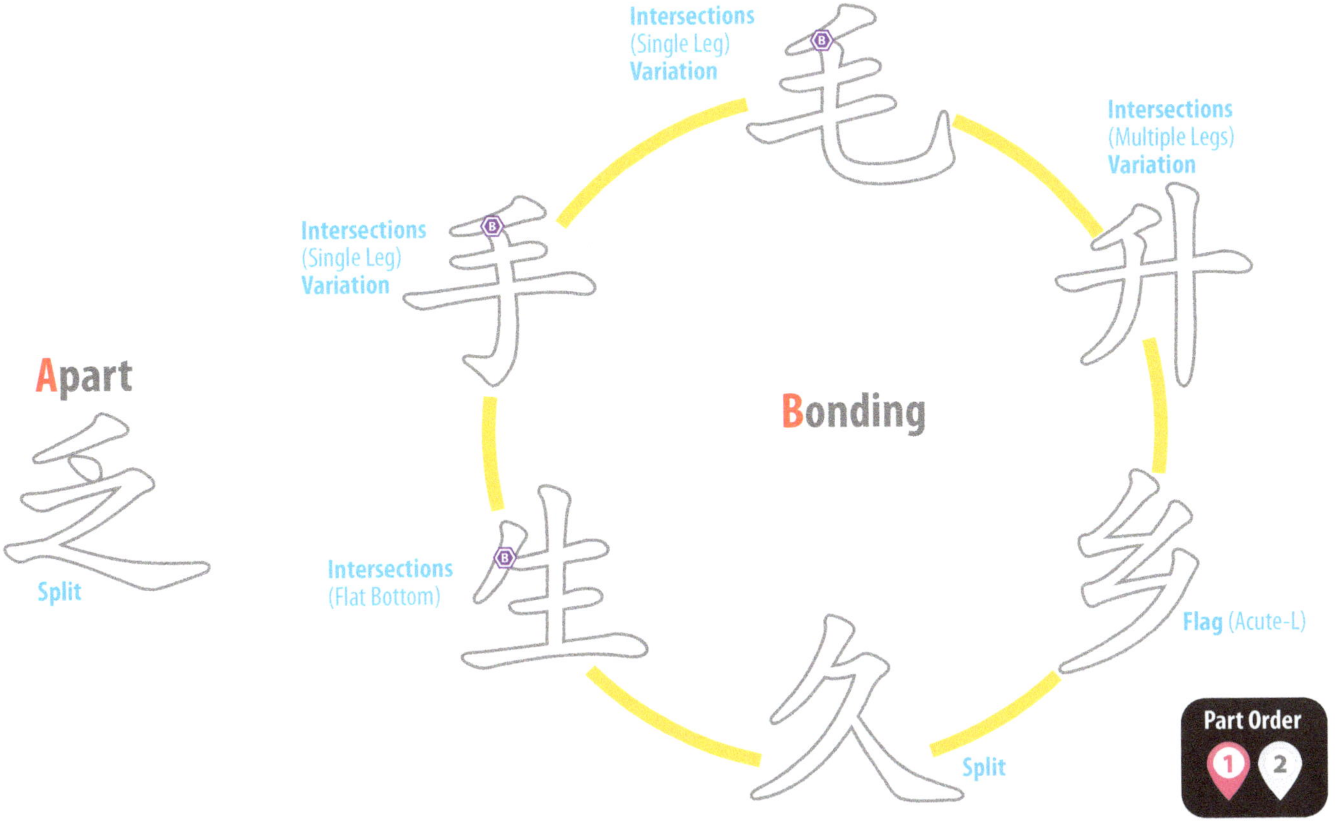

Intersections
(Single Leg)
Variation

毛

Intersections
(Multiple Legs)
Variation

升

Intersections
(Single Leg)
Variation

手

Bonding

Apart

乏

Split

久

Intersections
(Flat Bottom)

生

乡

Flag (Acute-L)

Split

Part Order
1 2

Activity 8

Colour these two-part characters (**L-Hook and qTRAIL alphabet**) according to the colours given, moving from **top down** or from **left to right**. The qTRAIL alphabet is named in each character. Look up the qTRAILS if you are unsure.

Apart

Final Dot Variation

Intersections (Flat Bottom) **Variation**

Activity 9

Colour these two-part characters (**L7-Hook and qTRAIL alphabet**) according to the colours given, moving from **top down** or from **left to right**. The qTRAIL alphabet is named in each character. Look up the qTRAILS if you are unsure.

Flipped C-Frame   **Perpendicular** (T-Shape)

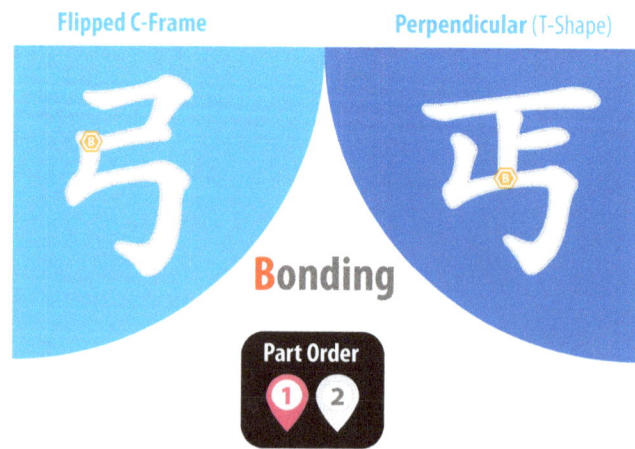

Bonding

Activity 10
A Stroke of Difference

Each character on the left can be matched to a character on the right by adding a stroke **'RL-Slash'**. Match the different pairs of characters and colour the characters on the right using the Part Order Colour Code. See example below.

Part Order
① ②

Activity 11
More Than A Stroke of Difference

Each character on the left can be matched to a character on the right by adding some strokes. Match the different pairs of characters and colour the characters on the right using the Part Order Colour Code. See example below.

巾
弓

几
幺

午
白

万
下

市
下

牛
玄

方
引

亢
百

Part Order
1 2 3

Top to **B**ottom

1
2

Previous section is about combining an alphabet and a stroke. Now we look into combining two alphabets from top to bottom. They can be **A**part or **B**onded to each other.

Observe
- How each alphabet adapts itself *(e.g. flattens)* to fit into the box

- The space occupied by each alphabet

(B) Alphabet + *Alphabet*

2 Alphabets

On the next page, the **2 Alphabets** in each character are positioned **Apart** from each other from **T2B**.

Adaptation

Observe the alphabets on the next page. Notice how the the alphabets change their sizes to 'squeeze' into the fixed space. They have to adapt by '**flattening**' themselves.

Space Distribution

Notice that the **distribution** of space for each alphabet in the character varies in the fixed-size box. For many characters, the two alphabets do not occupy equal space. Often it depends on the number of strokes within the alphabet and the shape of the alphabet.

(A) Distinct Boundaries

For some characters, the alphabets have distinct boundaries, that is they occupy spaces that do not overlap one another. A line can be drawn between them.

(B) Overlapping Space

In contrast, there are also characters that have alphabets occupying spaces that overlap each other. Like characters with distinct boundaries, the alphabets are also apart (not touching each other) but they do not flatten as much as those with distinct boundaries.

只 吕 呈 羊

T2B

(A) Distinct Space Boundaries

具 共 吉 台

▲

(B) Overlapping Space

冬 仑 公 多

欠 贝 见

Activity 12

These characters are made up of two alphabets placed Apart or Bonded to each other. Develop the ability to identify the alphabets. Refer to the qTRAILS map (pages 206 - 209) if needed.

Colour the two alphabets in each character from **TOP to BOTTOM** using the given colour code.

爻　名　冗　艾　兄

备　父　弄　吞　甾

Part Order
① ②

奉　介　支　节

L2R **L**eft to **R**ight

Combine two alphabets from left to right, **A**part from each other.

Observe
- How each alphabet adapts itself *(e.g. slims down)* to fit into the box

- The space occupied by each alphabet

(B) Alphabet + *Alphabet*

2 Alphabets

In this section, the **2 Alphabets** in each character are positioned **A**part from each other from **L2R**

Adaptation

Note the alphabet on the left of a character does not intrude into the space of alphabet on the right of the character. The alphabets have to change their sizes to 'squeeze' into the fixed space. This time they have to adapt by slimming down and/or shortening or tilting or slanting a stroke.

Read more about Adaptation in on page 185 and in LCWW1.

Part Order **1** **2**

Activity 13

These characters are made up of two alphabets. Develop the ability to identify the alphabets. Refer to the qTRAILS map if needed.

Colour these two-part characters from LEFT TO RIGHT using the given colour code.

Pre-test: Guess the Paths

The paths show the Part Order of characters, showing which part to be written first, second and so on. Match the characters to the paths (in the middle). See example. Colour the parts to make the Part Order easier to visualise

 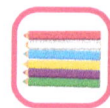

Paths

型　伤

盐　盖

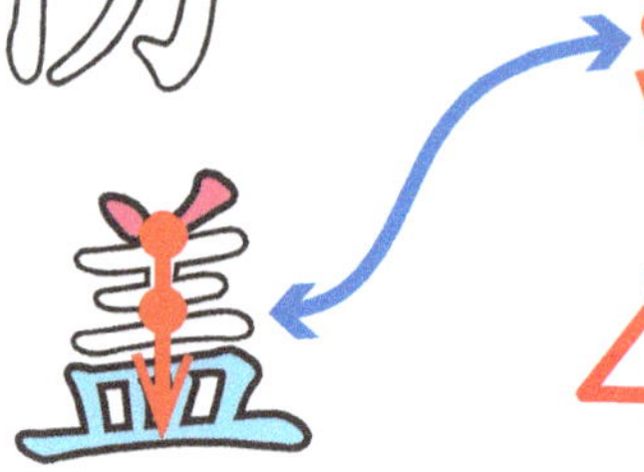

劲　胡

梆　别

　　芳

呛　规

箱　崩

壳　能

昂　范

Answers will be revealed later. Look out for them.

T2B — Top to Bottom

Continuing from the previous section, now add a part to the top or bottom of a 2-part T2B character. When more parts are added, they will stack on top of one another. These parts can be **A**part from or **B**onded to one another.

Observe

- How each part adapts itself *(e.g. flattens)* to fit into the box

- The space occupied by each part

(C) Alphabet(s) + *Stroke(s)*

T2B TRIPLET

Answers to the pre-test:

Activity 14

Part(s) are added at the top of the first character to form the second character in each pair. Compare the two characters and identify the common parts. Colour the second character from TOP TO BOTTOM using the given colour code.

Note there are 4 parts in this character.

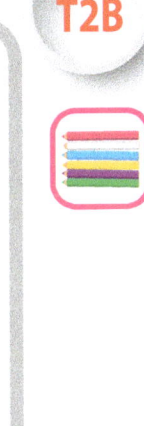

Part Order
1 2 3 4

Activity 15

Part(s) are added at the top or bottom of the first character to form the second character in each pair. Compare the two characters and identify the common parts. Colour the second character from TOP TO BOTTOM using the given colour code.

Part Order
1 2 3 4 5 6

Activity 16

Observe how different characters are formed when different parts are added to the same character. Compare each set of characters and identify the common parts. Colour the characters in each set from TOP TO BOTTOM using the given colour code.

Part Order
1 2 3 4 5 6

Note there are only 4 parts in this character!

Activity 17

Identify the alphabets and strokes in the characters and colour them from top to bottom using the Part Order Colour Code.

Part Order 1 2 3 4

50　　**RULE 1: T2R / L2R**

Activity 18

T2B

These characters are all written from top to bottom. Your job is to identify the alphabets and strokes in the characters and colour them from **TOP TO BOTTOM** according to the Part Order Colour Code. Refer to the qTRAILS Map (pages 206 - 209) in the Answer section if you are not sure of the alphabets.

Alphabets + Strokes

育

章

韋

寮

益

寅

嘗

竟

鼻

亭

寬

膏

贲

奚

荒

睿

Part Order
1 2 3 4 5 6

L2R Left to Right

Continuing from the previous section, now add a
part to the left or right of a 2-part L2R character. The
parts will squeeze into the fixed size box side by
side. Note these parts are **A**part from one another.

Observe

- How each part adapts itself *(e.g. slims down)*
  to fit into the box

- The space occupied by each part

(C) Alphabet(s) + *Stroke(s)*

L2R TRIPLET

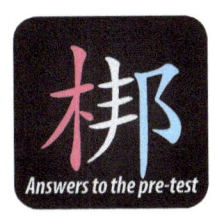

Answers to the pre-test

Activity 19

A part is added to the **left, right or middle** of the first character to form the second character. Compare each pair of characters and identify the common parts. Colour the second character in each pair from **LEFT TO RIGHT** according to the Part Order Colour Code.

Part Order
1 2 3

L2R

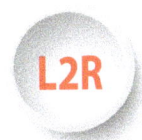

Activity 20

Parts in these characters are written from left to right. Identify the alphabets and strokes in the characters and colour them from **LEFT TO RIGHT** according to the Part Order Colour Code. Refer to the qTRAILS Map in the Answer section if you are not sure of the alphabets.

Alphabets + Strokes
Up to 4 Parts

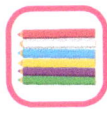

亿 刊
以 犯

卧 帅
拒 淋

班 耕
排 冲

Part Order

1 2 3 4

Adaptation of Parts: Flatten

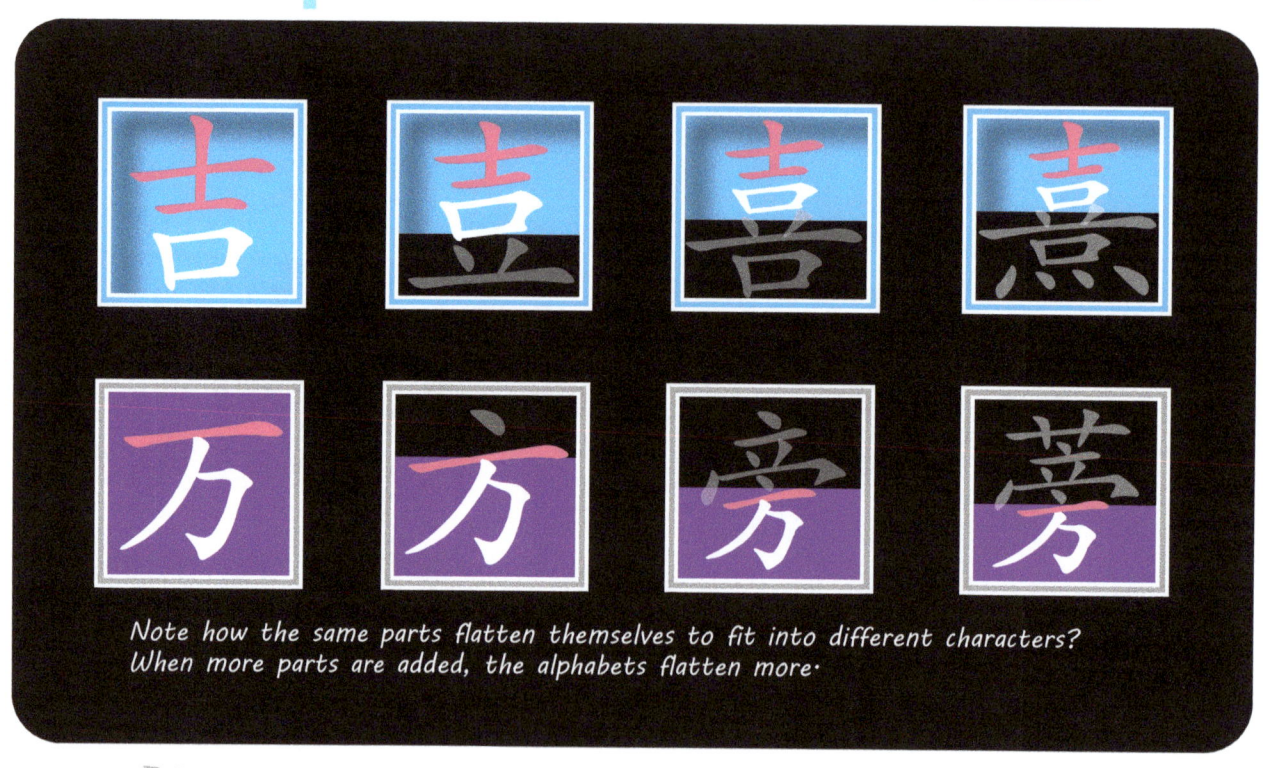

Note how the same parts flatten themselves to fit into different characters? When more parts are added, the alphabets flatten more.

Combi

T2B & L2R

(A) Triplets

(B) Quartets

Combi

Acute-L / Acute-7

Many characters can be written using T2R and L2R rules combined. This section shows how characters with 3 parts can be arranged within the square box by adding a part to the top or bottom of a 2-part L2R character.

Observe

- How the structure of a character changes when a part is added to its top or bottom

- How each part adapts itself *(e.g. flattens, or shrinks)* to fit into the box.

(C) Alphabet(s) + *Stroke(s)*

ACUTE-L / ACUTE-7 TRIPLETS

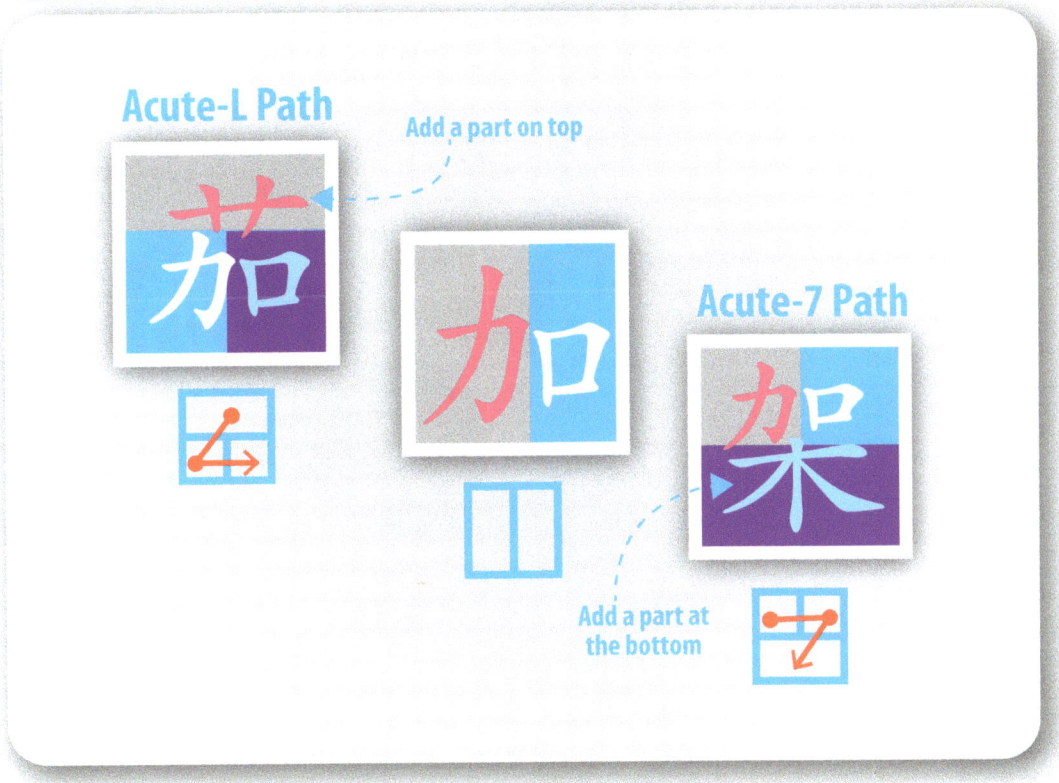

Acute-L Path

Add a part on top

茄

加

Acute-7 Path

架

Add a part at the bottom

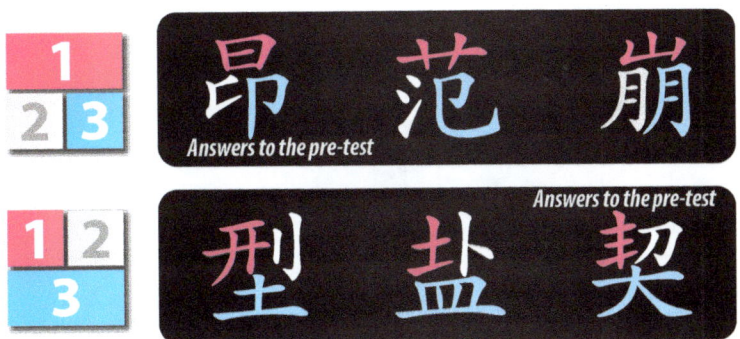

Answers to the pre-test

昂　范　崩

Answers to the pre-test

型　盐　契

Activity 21

Compare each pair of characters and identify the common parts. Colour the second character in each pair in the correct Part Order using the given colour code.

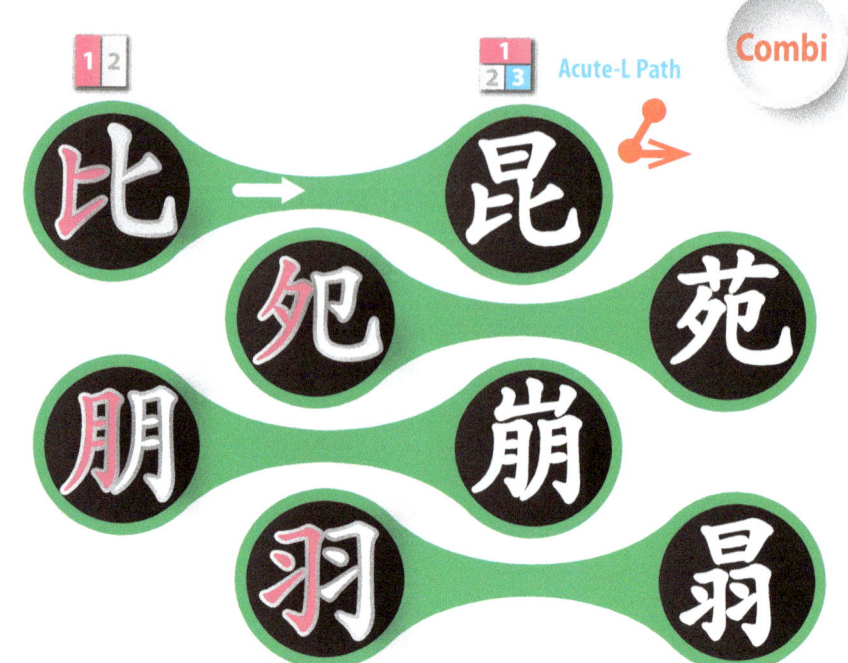

Combi

Inverted-V Path / V-Path

More characters are written using T2R and L2R rules combined. This section shows how characters with 3 parts can be arranged within the square box by adding a part to the left or right of a 2-part T2B character.

Observe

- How the structure of a character changes when a part is added to its left or right

- How each part adapts itself *(e.g. slims down or shrinks)* to fit into the box.

(C) Alphabet(s) + *Stroke(s)*

V-PATH / INVERTED-V PATH TRIPLETS

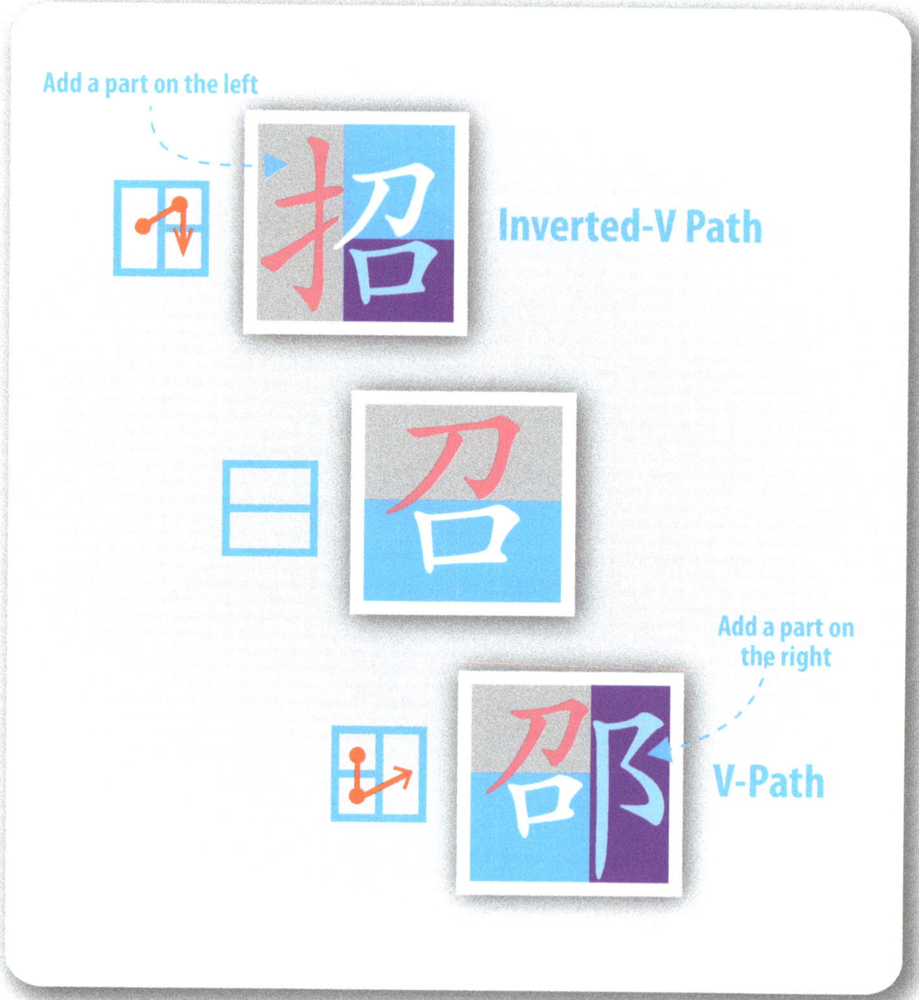

Add a part on the left

招 Inverted-V Path

召

Add a part on the right

邵 V-Path

Inverted-V Path
V-Path

Inverted-V Path

V-Path

Activity 22

Compare each pair of characters and identify the common parts. Colour the second character in each pair in the correct Part Order using the given colour code.

Observe how the parts adapt to fit into the space.

Part Order
1 2 3

Activity 23

Observe how characters change when different parts are added to different sides of the same character. Colour the characters in each set in the correct Part Order using the given colour code. Observe how the parts adapt to fit into the space.

Combi

萌

盟

畦

郑

明

圭

关

化

卦

华

花

联

Part Order
1 2 3

Inverted-N Path / Z-Path

These characters are formed by 4 parts. Although they look similar, the paths to write the parts are very different. One moves downwards first before moving rightwards while the other moves rightwards first before moving downwards.

Observe

- The parts in each type of quartet

- How each part adapts itself *(e.g. shrinks)* to fit into the box.

(C) Alphabet(s) + *Stroke(s)*

日 钅 欠 日

↓

钦

Inverted-N Path

能

1	3
2	4

冂 双

ᴢ 叕

Z-Path

1	2
3	4

箱

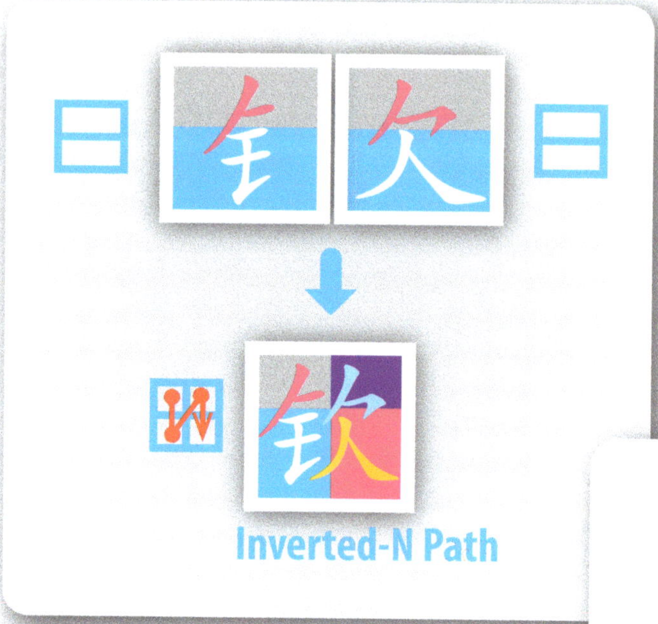

Activity 24

Observe how these characters transform into Quartets by adding parts to them. Colour the characters in the correct Part Order using the given colour code. Observe how the parts adapt to fit into the space.

Combi

Inverted-N Path
Z-Path

苗 锚

肋 筋

冬 终

直 殖

扣 箔

竹 饰 翡 琵 箱

Part Order
1 2 3 4

Activity 25

Observe how these characters transform into Triplets by adding parts to them.

Compare each set of characters and identify the common parts. Colour the characters in each set in the correct Part Order using the given colour code. Observe how the parts adapt to fit into the space.

Part Order
1 2 3

Combi

Activity 26

Observe how these characters transform into Triplets by adding parts to them. Compare each set of characters and identify the common parts. Colour the characters in each set in the correct Part Order using the given colour code. Observe how the parts adapt to fit into the space.

Part Order
1 2 3 4 5

Activity 27

Draw a line to match the **character** to the **structure** that shows the Part Order of the character.

Combi

(1) 1 2  3

(2) 1 / 2 3

(3) 1 2 / 3

枮

表

宦

組

帯

故

留

临

笳

段

(4) 1 / 2 / 3

(5) 1 2 / 3 4

(6) 1 3 / 2 4

(7) 1 / 2 3

(8) 1 / 2 3

M4S

Middle before Sides

(A) Inverted-V Dots

(B) 'V Dots'

(C) Vertical Dots

(D) Miscellaneous

Middle before Sides

This section shows exceptions to the L2R rule. Instead of writing from left to right, these characters are written first in the middle, follwed by the left side then the right side.

For each set of characters, observe
- The common parts on the left and right sides (e.g. Inverted-V Dots)

- The middle part(s) which are different

M4S These characters have dots arranged like an inverted-V on the sides. Observe the different **middle part(s)**. The names of these alphabets and strokes are labelled.

Dots by the sides: Inverted-V Dots

Vertical Left

2 1 3

Parts 2 and 3 belong to the same alphabet

小 忝

3 parts

2 1 3

Intersection
(Single Leg)
[qTRAIL: 8V]

杀 余

Perpendicular
(T-Shape)
Variations
[qTRAIL: 6V]

示 亦

7-Frame
[qTRAIL: 22]

办

These characters have dots arranged like a V-shape on the sides. Observe the different **middle part(s)**. The names of these alphabets and strokes are labelled.

Dots by the sides: **V Dots**

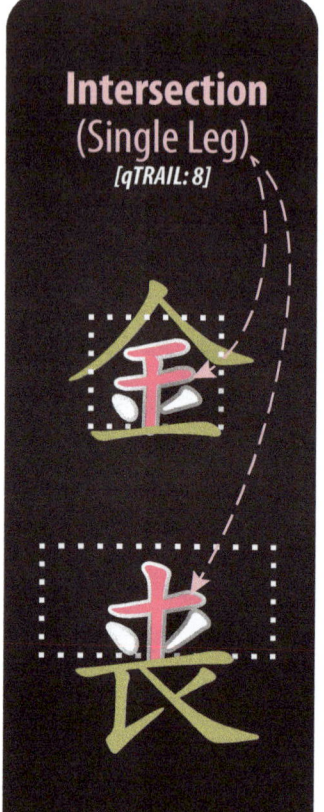

Intersection
(Single Leg)
[qTRAIL: 8]

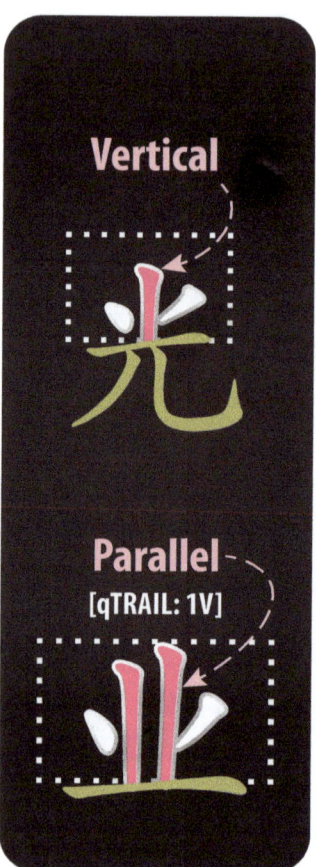

Vertical

Parallel
[qTRAIL: 1V]

Perpendicular
(T-Shape)
[qTRAIL: 6]

Dots by the sides: **Vertical Dots**

Vertical Dots

Vertical Left

泰

[qTRAIL: 3]

2 1 3

Split
[qTRAIL: 13]

脊

These three characters have two sets of **vertical dots** (which are written T2B) on the two sides. Observe the different **middle part(s)**. The names of these alphabets and strokes are labelled.

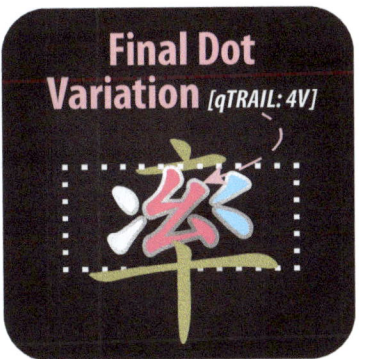

Final Dot Variation *[qTRAIL: 4V]*

率

These three characters have an alphabet from the 'Slide' qTRAILS on the right side. Observe the different **middle part(s)**. The names of these alphabets or strokes are labelled.

Slide (right)

On the right side: **Slide**

Vertical Left

水

[qTRAIL: 15]

Vertical Left

录

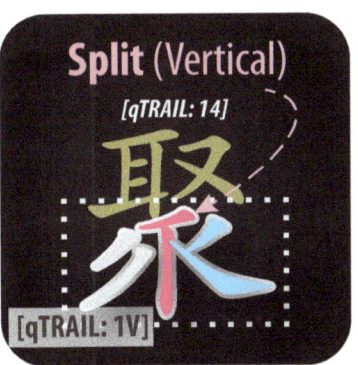

Split (Vertical)
[qTRAIL: 14]

聚

[qTRAIL: 1V]

M4S

These characters have different alphabets in the middle and by the sides Observe the **parts** coloured in the Part Order Colour Code. The names of these alphabets are labelled.

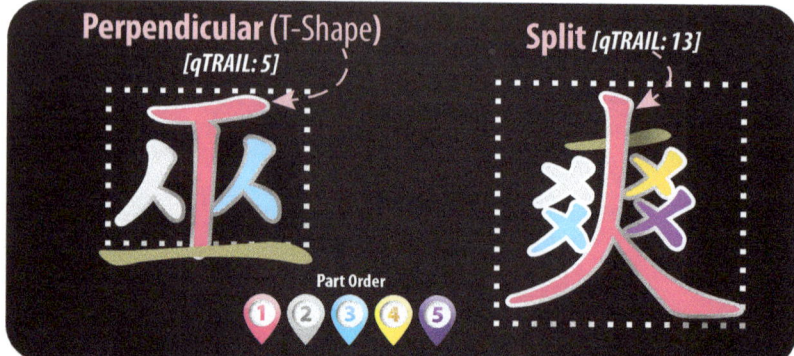

Miscellaneous

Split / Crosses
by the sides

Perpendicular (T-Shape)
[qTRAIL: 5]

Split *[qTRAIL: 13]*

Part Order
① ② ③ ④ ⑤

Miscellaneous

Intersection
(Single Leg)
[qTRAIL: 1]

L-Frame on the right

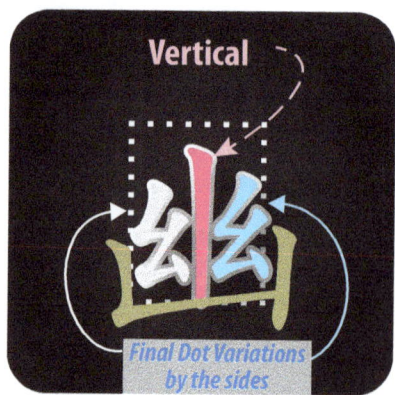

Vertical

Final Dot Variations by the sides

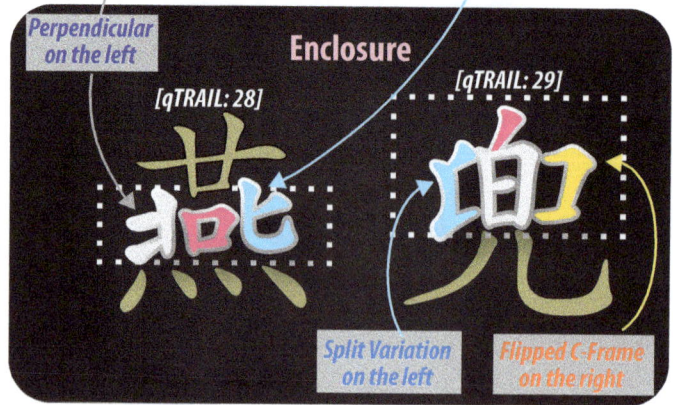

Perpendicular on the left

Enclosure
[qTRAIL: 28]   *[qTRAIL: 29]*

Split Variation on the left   *Flipped C-Frame on the right*

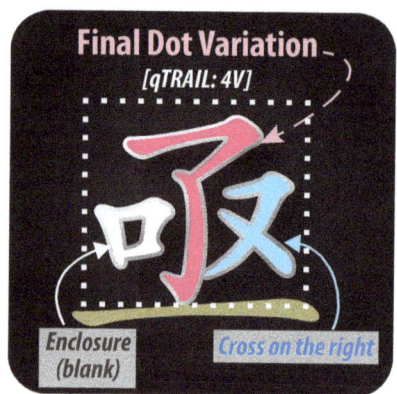

Final Dot Variation
[qTRAIL: 4V]

Enclosure (blank)   *Cross on the right*

Activity 28

Colour the characters in the correct Part Order according to the Part Order Colour Code.

Part Order
1 2 3 4 5

7 PART ORDER RULES

03

S4M

Sides before Middle

(A) Inverted-V Dots

(B) Splits

Sides before Middle

Another exception to the L2R and M4S rules, characters following this rule are written first by the sides follwed by the middle part(s).

For each set of characters, observe
- The common parts on the left and right sides (e.g. Inverted-V Dots)

- The middle part(s) which are different

These characters are written on the sides first, followed by the middle. Each character, except the last one, has two dots arranged like a **V-shape**. Observe the **middle part(s)** coloured in the Part Order Colour Code. The names of these alphabets and strokes are labelled.

Dots by the sides: Inverted-V Dots

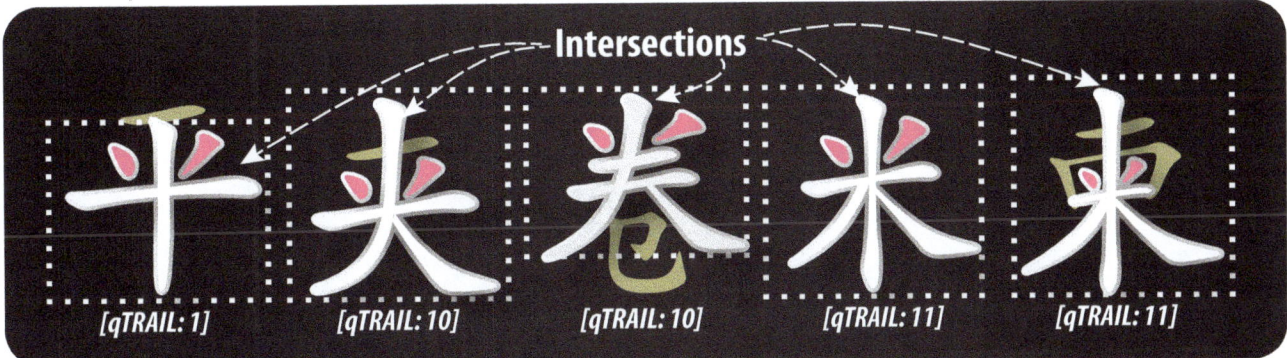

Intersections

平 [qTRAIL: 1]　夫 [qTRAIL: 10]　卷 [qTRAIL: 10]　米 [qTRAIL: 11]　東 [qTRAIL: 11]

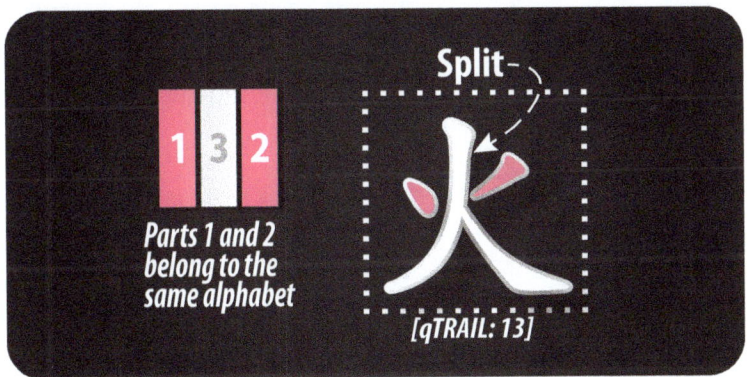

Split

1 3 2

Parts 1 and 2 belong to the same alphabet

火 [qTRAIL: 13]

Splits by the sides

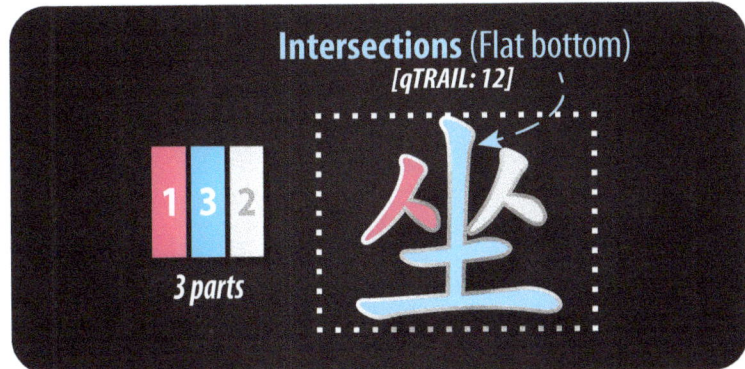

Intersections (Flat bottom)
[qTRAIL: 12]

1 3 2

3 parts

坐

Activity 29

Draw an arrow to the left or right to classify these characters according to the **Part Order of the parts outlined in green**. See example.

S4M Sides before Middle

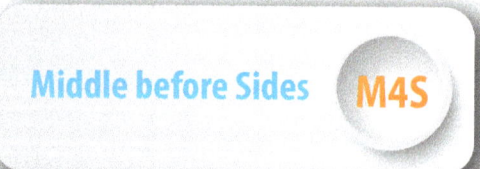

Part Order 1 2 3 4 5 6

Middle before Sides **M4S**

灰 ← 灰

显

筮

常

宗

番

並

鉴

券

挫

尖

严

黑

Activity 30

Round up the characters in the given shapes to classify them according to the Part Order of the parts outlined in **orange**. Colour the parts in the corect Part Order according to the given colour code.

S4M ▢ — Sides before Middle

Combi ⬡ — Left to Right / Top to Bottom

M4S ◯ — Middle before Sides

Part Order
① ② ③ ④ ⑤ ⑥

承　脊　率　燕

街　脊　炎

亲　尝　兜　爽　半

座　　樊　聚　伞

掰　来　炼　聚　乘

Activity 31

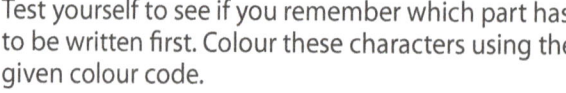

Test yourself to see if you remember which part has to be written first. Colour these characters using the given colour code.

7 PART ORDER RULES

04

041

Outside before Inside

(A) 7-Frame
(B) Inverse 7-Frame
(C) L-Frame
(D) n-Frame

O4I **O**utside before **I**nside

These characters are enclosed on two or three sides. The frames that surround them look like number 7 or Inverse-7 or English letters L or n.

Observe
- The different types of frames made up by single stroke (e.g. 7-Hook) or alphabets.

O41

Take note of the **2-sided frames** that enclose like the number 7. The frame is written first before the part enclosed by the frame is written.

SINGLE STROKE

7-Hook

7-Leanback

Double-7 Hook

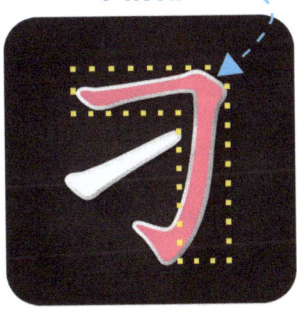

qTRAIL ALPHABET

Split Variation
[qTRAILS: 14]

Observe the 2-sided frames that enclose like a laterally-inverted number 7. Observe the frames made up of different combinations of **Horizontal**, **RL-Slash**, **Vertical** and **Vertical Right**.

Inverse 7-Frame

Perpendicular (Variation) *[qTRAILS: 6V]*

Intersection (Variation) *[qTRAILS: 8V]*

Split *[qTRAILS: 14]*

Split (Variation) *[qTRAILS: 14V]*

More Variations

In these characters the Inverse-7 Frames, with 3 or more strokes, look more complicated.

Intersection (Variation) *[qTRAILS: 8V]*

Part Order
① ② ③ ④ ⑤ ⑥

Perpendicular (Variation) *[qTRAILS: 6V]*

Observe the **2-sided frames** that enclose like the letter L. Identify the parts in these characters. Refer to the qTRAILS Map if needed.

L-Frame

[qTRAILS 18]

[qTRAILS 17]

Compare the following characters with characters in the next section (I4O rule) which have the same structure but are written in the opposite sequence.

More Variations

Part Order
① ② ③ ④ ⑤ ⑥

Take note of the **3-sided frames** that enclose like the small letter n. The frame is written first before the part within.

[qTRAILS 28]

[qTRAILS 28V]

[qTRAILS 28]

More Variations

Part Order

Activity 32

Colour the parts in the corect Part Order according to the given colour code.

041

后 勾
周

左 勾
冏

存
凤 见

冈 司
反 不 厓 网

Part Order
1 2 3

Activity 33

Colour the parts in the corect Part Order according to the given colour code.

041

同 赴 爪 虏

危 览 题 店

布 责 槛 寇

应 痒 贞 度

Part Order

1 2 3 4 5 6

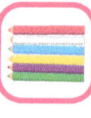

140

Inside before Outside

(A) L-Frames

(B) U-Frame

I4O   **I**nside before **O**utside

These characters are enclosed on two or three sides. The frames that surround them look like English letters L or U. They are written in the opposite sequence of those in the previous rule.

Observe
- The types of frames made up of single stroke (e.g. L-Bend) or alphabets

140

In these characters, the parts enclosed by the frames are written before the frame. Observe the 2-sided frames. Compare the following characters with characters in the previous section (O4I rule) which have the same structure but are written in the opposite sequence.

L-Bend

L-Frame
(Split)

[qTRAILS 13]

L-Frame
Cross)

[qTRAILS 16]

U-Frame

[qTRAILS 27]

Activity 34

Colour the parts in the corect Part Order according to the given colour code.

Part Order
1 2 3 4

Activity 35

Round up the characters in the given shapes to classify them according to the Part Order of the parts.outlined in **blue.**
Colour the parts in the corect Part Order according to the given colour code.

140 Inside before Outside

Outside before Inside 041

这 随 咎 遨

馗 趁 击 彪

迷 翅 遴 筵

毯 函 继 延

Part Order
1 2 3 4 5 6

OIO

Outside-Inside-Outside

(A) Inverse 7-Frame

(B) C-Frame

(C) 7-Frame and L-Frame

(D) Enclosure

OIO

Outside Inside Outside

These characters are enclosed on two, three or four sides. Parts of the frames are built before the inside and then other parts of the frames are built to surround the parts inside.

Observe

- How the frames are created

- The Bond Points and/or Cross Points on the frames

In these characters, build part of the frame first, fill inside then build another part of the frame. The components that make up the frames are named.

Horizontal

Vertical Left

Horizontal

Leanback

Intersection
(Flat Bottom)
[qTRAIL: 12]

Exception
(Cross)
[qTRAIL: 16E]

Exception (Cross) intersects **Perpendicular Variations**

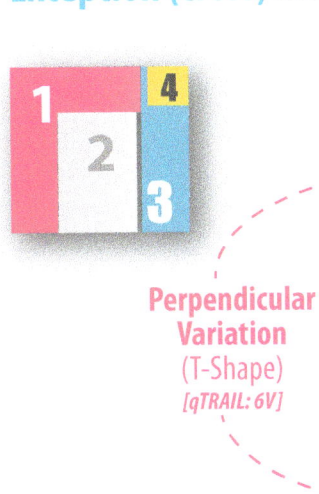

Perpendicular Variation
(T-Shape)
[qTRAIL: 6V]

Exception
(Cross)
[qTRAIL: 16E]

This three-sided frame enclose like the English alphabet 'C', with an opening on the right.

C-Frame

Horizontal bonds with L-Bend

Perpendicular (T-Shape) bonds with L-Bend

Perpendicular
(T-Shape)
[qTRAIL: 6]

OIO

In this character, you have to combine a 7-frame and a L-frame. Note that these frames are not touching each other.

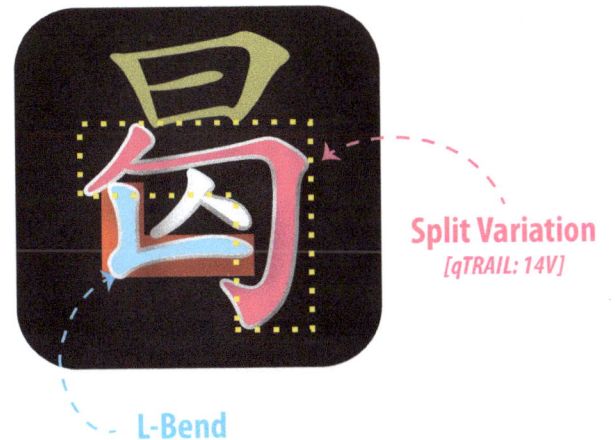

Split Variation
[qTRAIL: 14V]

L-Bend

n-Frame bonds with Horizontal

n-Frame
[qTRAIL: 28]

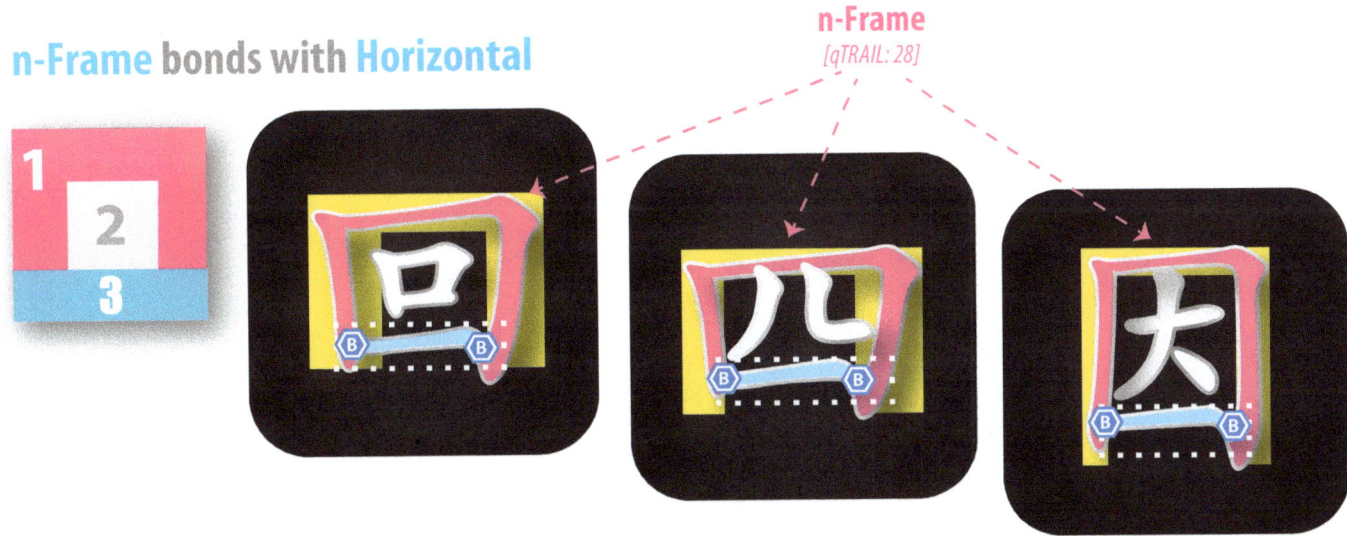

Colour the PARTS in the correct Part Order according to the given colour code.

OIO

Part Order
1 2 3 4 5 6

FPF

Flag Pole First

(A) Flipped C-Frame

Flag Pole First

These characters each has a pole with two Flipped C-Frames attached to it.

Observe
- The 'poles' in different characters

- The relative size of the Flipped C-Frames in each character

Flipped C-Frame

Flipped C-Frames bond with Vertical or Split (Vertical)

Vertical

Flipped
C-Frames
[qTRAILS: 21]

Split
(with Vertical)
[qTRAILS: 14]

Flipped
C-Frames
[qTRAILS: 21]

Colour the PARTS in the correct Part Order according to the given colour code.

FPF

Part Order
1 2 3 4 5 6

7 PART ORDER RULES

06

FPL

Flag Pole Last

(A) Flipped C-Frame

F_{lag} P_{ole} L_{ast}

These characters have a Flipped C-Frame each.

Observe

- The 'poles' in different characters

- The different types of Flipped C-Frames

- The parts (if any) (the 3rd part) enclosed

Flipped C-Frame bonds with RL-Slash or Split or L-Hook or Perpendicular

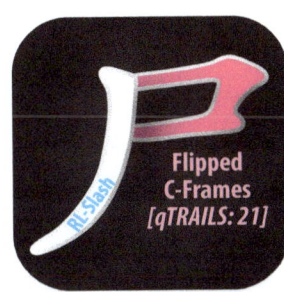

Flipped C-Frames [qTRAILS: 21] — RL-Slash

Split

L-Hook

L-Hook

Perpendicular (Half Ladder) [qTRAILS: 5]

Flipped C-Frame bonds with RL-Slash or Vertical Right

L-Frame [qTRAILS: 27] — RL-Slash

Interaction Variation [qTRAILS: 8V] — Vertical Right

Slide [qTRAILS: 15] — Vertical Right

Activity 38

Colour the PARTS in the correct Part Order according to the given colour code.

FPL

Part Order
1 2 3 4 5

DOF

Dot(s) First

(A) Top / Top-Left Corner

DOF Dot(s) First

These characters have dot(s) positioned at the top or top-left corner. These dots are written first before other parts.

Observe
- The position of the dot(s) in the characters

DOF

DOL

Dot(s) Last

(A) Right Side
(B) Left / Centre / Bottom

Dot(s) Last

The dot(s) in these characters are positioned at other places other than the top and top-left corners. These dots are written last after other parts are written.

Observe
- The position of the dot(s) in the characters

Left or Centre or Bottom

Opening at the bottom

Activity 39

Colour the PARTS in the correct Part Order according to the given colour code.

DOF DOL

Part Order
1 2 3 4 5 6

Activity 40

Round up the characters in the given shapes to classify them according to the Part Order of the parts highlighted in **green**. Colour the parts in the corect Part Order according to the given colour code.

Flag Pole Last

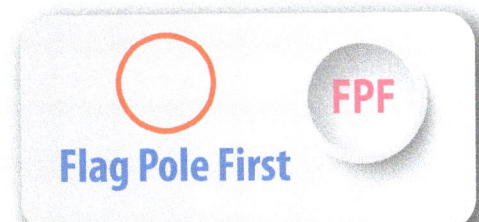

Flag Pole First

  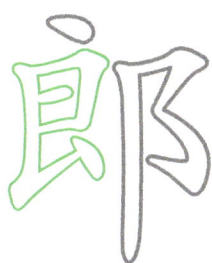

Activity 41

All the charcters have dot(s). Take note if the dot(s) is/are written first or last. Colour these characters in the correct Part Order according to the colour code.

戒 代 勺 书 飞

普 寒 耆 房

尽 庆 厌

Part Order
① 2 ③ ④ ⑤ ⑥

拔 拔 庄 压

然

雨 尉 煞 图

S2C
Simple to Complex

CHARACTERS WITH COMPLEX STRUCTURES

7 PART ORDER RULES

Simple to Complex

From the basic standard structures you have learnt in the '7 Part Order Rules', you can create characters with more complex structures by adding part(s) to characters with simple structures or combining simple structures.

Observe

- The position (e.g. top, bottom, left or right) the additional part(s) are added

- The change in colours in the characters when additional part(s) are added

- How simple structures can be combined to form characters with complex structures

Activity 42

In each pair of characters, the first character is written from **T2B**. A part is added to the **left or right** side of the first character. Colour the second character in the correct Part Order using the Part Order Colour Code.

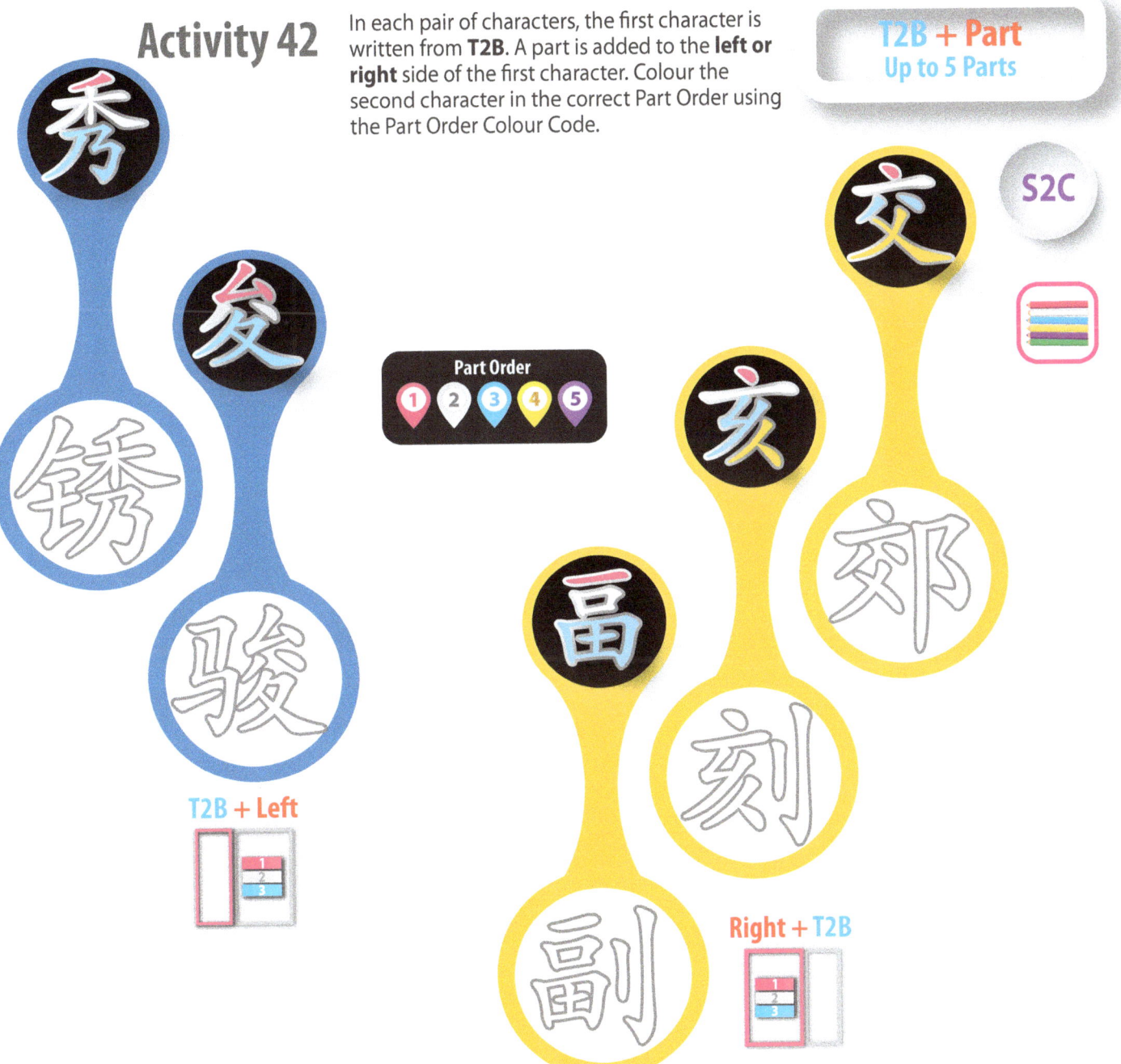

T2B + Part
Up to 5 Parts

S2C

Part Order
1 2 3 4 5

T2B + Left

Right + T2B

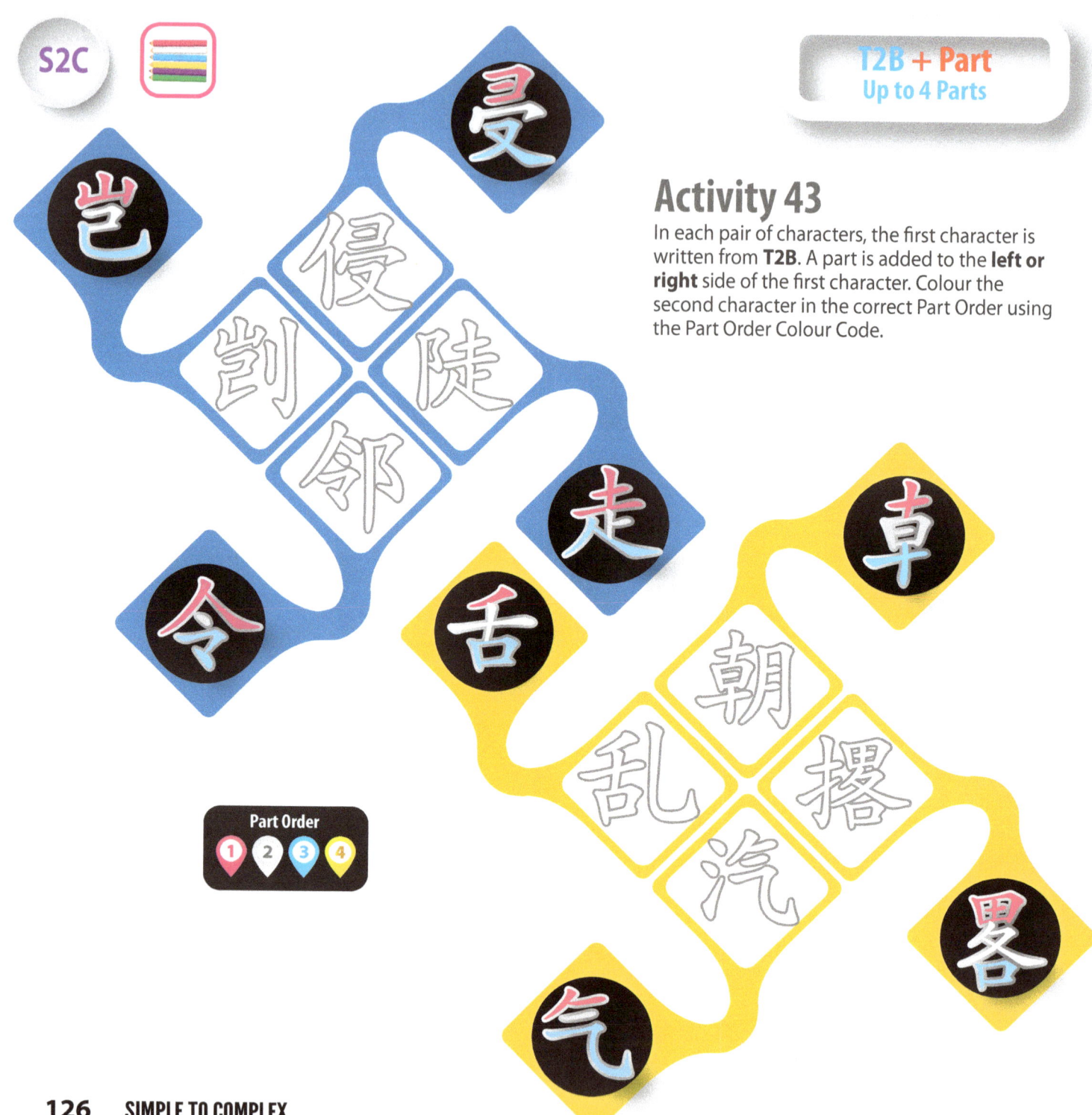

T2B + Part
Up to 4 Parts

Activity 43

In each pair of characters, the first character is written from **T2B**. A part is added to the **left or right** side of the first character. Colour the second character in the correct Part Order using the Part Order Colour Code.

Part Order
1 2 3 4

Activity 44

In each pair of characters, the first character is written from **T2B**. A part is added to the **left or right** side of the first character. Colour the second character in the correct Part Order using the Part Order Colour Code.

字 齐

勃 济 凌 授

受 亥 夋

享 郭 孩 幅 位

畐 立

Part Order
1 2 3 4 5

Activity 45

In each pair of characters, the first character is written from **T2B**. A part is added to the **left or right** side of the first character. Colour the second character in the correct Part Order using the Part Order Colour Code.

Part Order
1 2 3 4 5 6

Activity 46

Observe how the characters get more complex when parts are added to different sides of the characters. Colour the characters in the correct Part Order according to the Part Order Colour Code.

Part Order
1 2 3 4 5 6

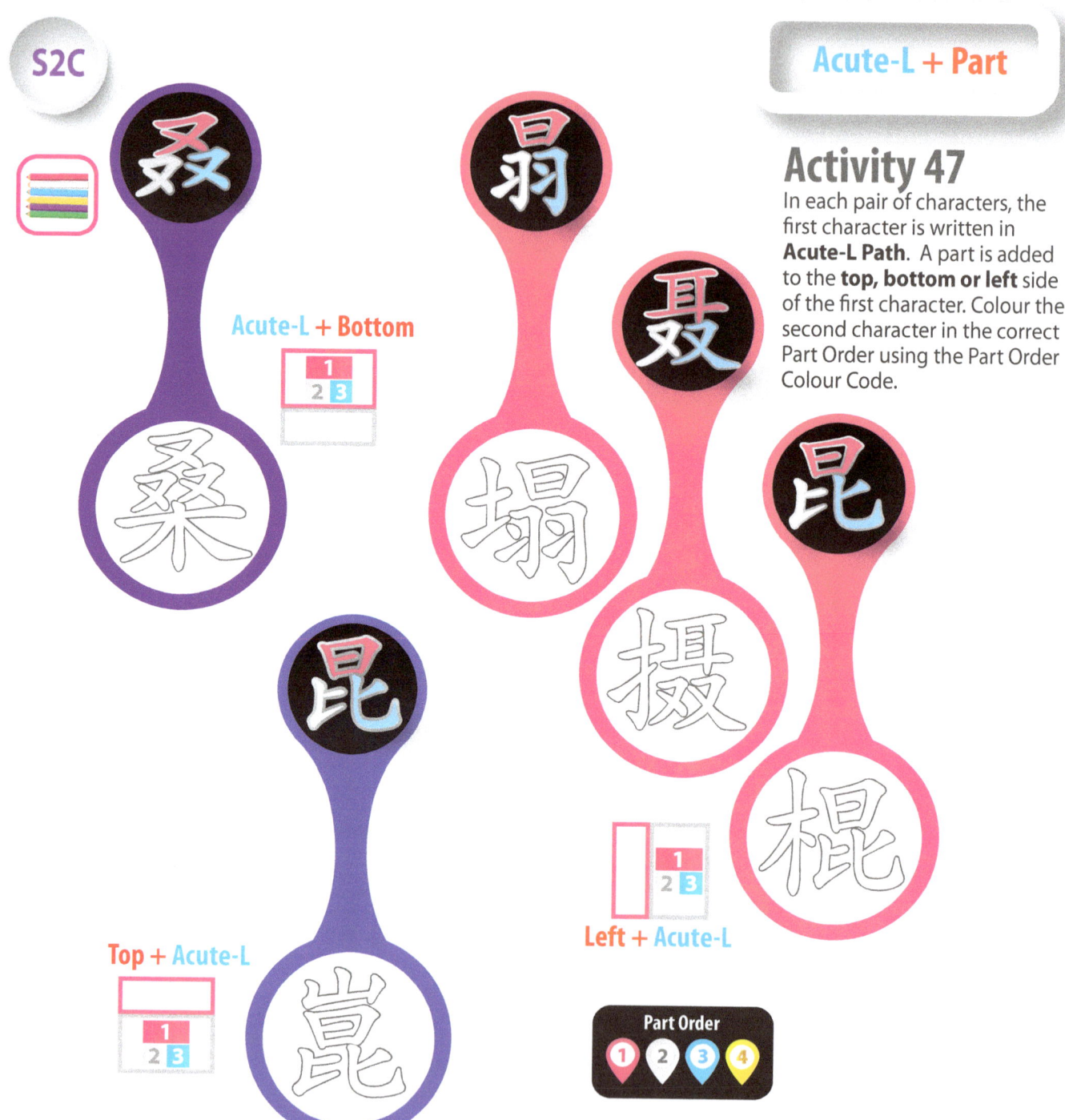

S2C

Acute-L + Bottom

1
2 3

Top + Acute-L

1
2 3

Left + Acute-L

1
2 3

Activity 47

In each pair of characters, the first character is written in **Acute-L Path**. A part is added to the **top, bottom or left** side of the first character. Colour the second character in the correct Part Order using the Part Order Colour Code.

Part Order
1 2 3 4

Activity 48

In each pair of characters, the first character is written in **Acute-7 Path**. A part is added to the **top or left** side of the first character. Colour the second character in the correct Part Order using the Part Order Colour Code.

Acute-7 + Part

Left + Acute-7

Acute-7 + Top

Part Order
1 2 3 4

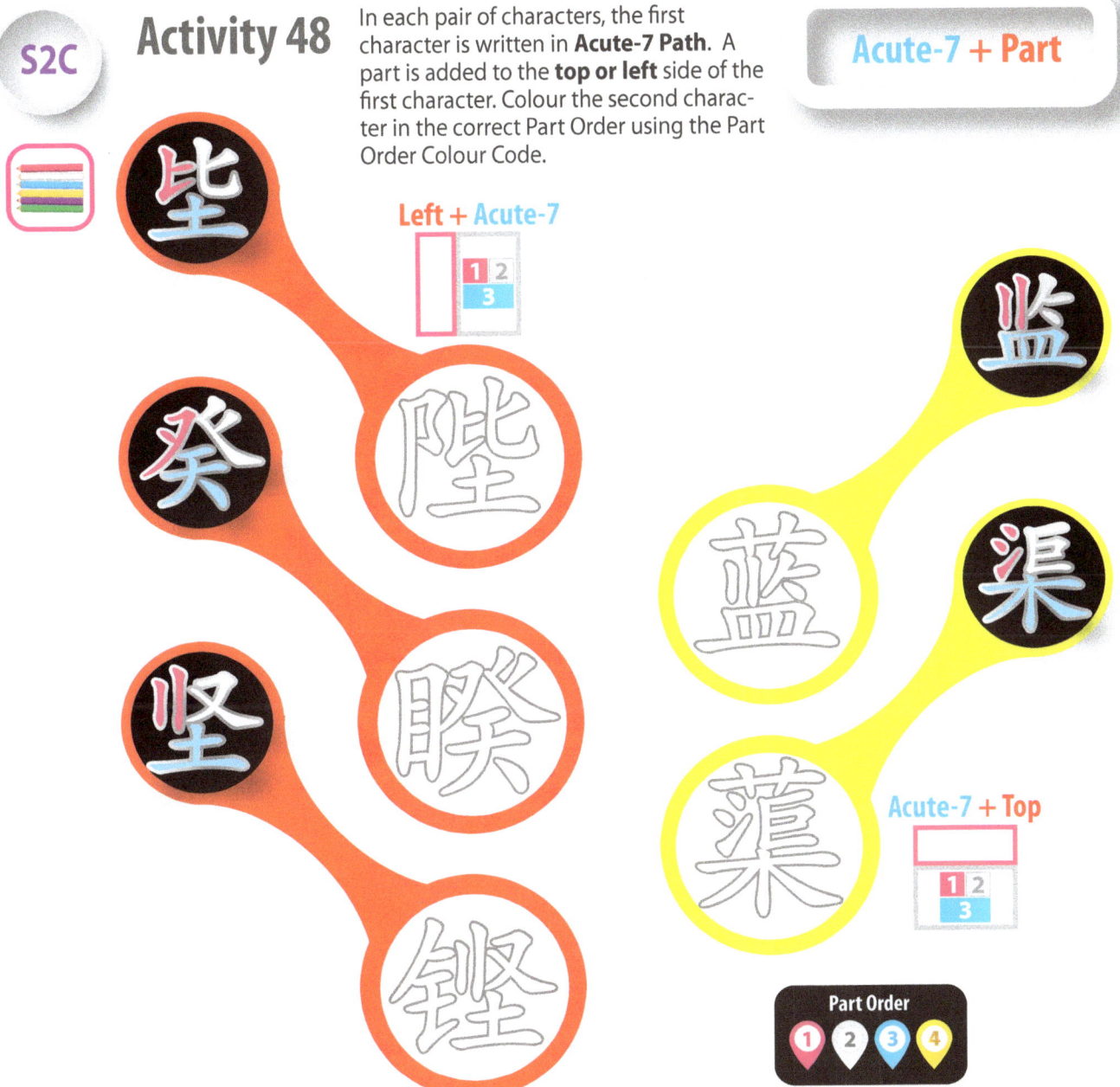

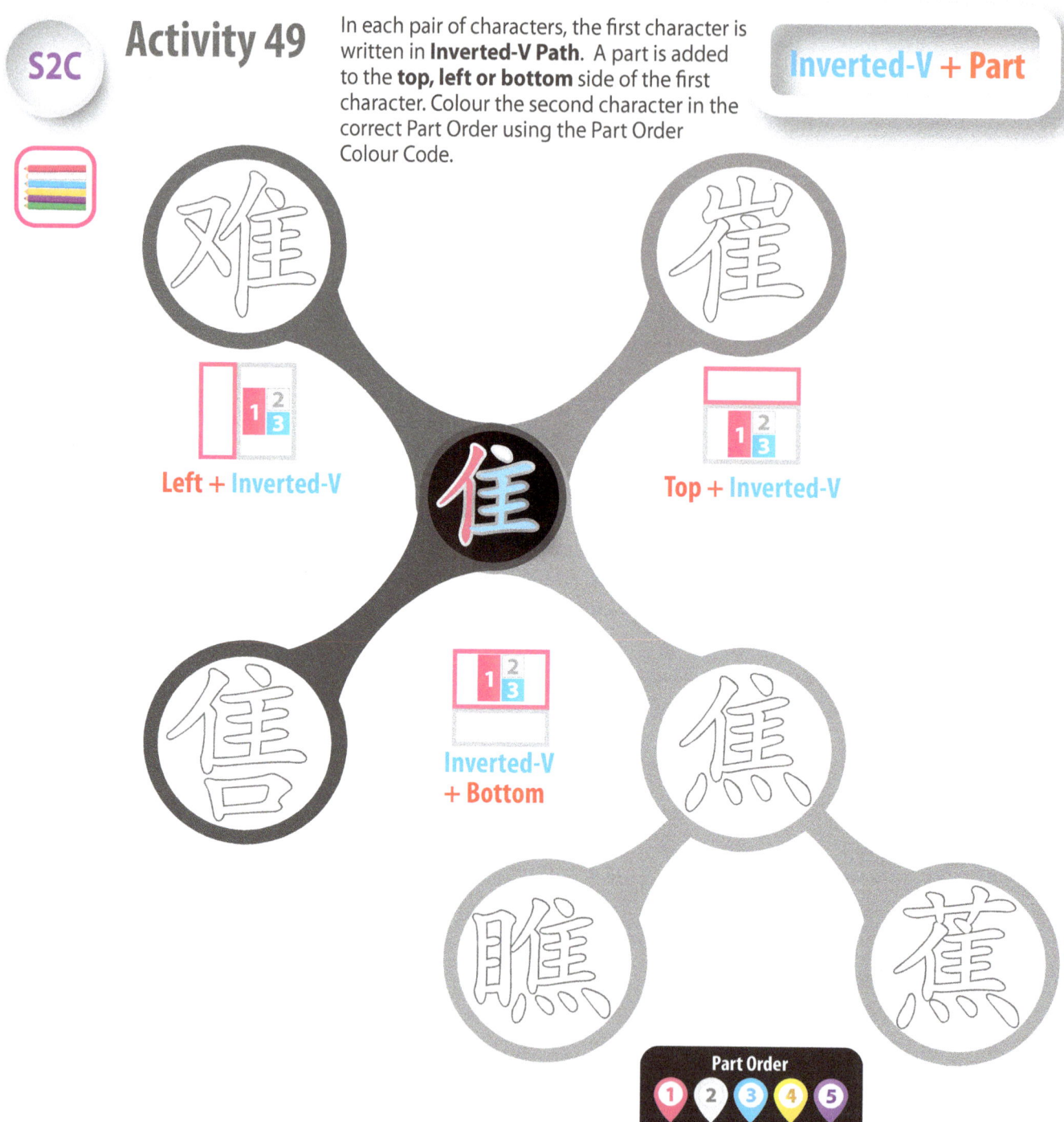

Activity 49

S2C

In each pair of characters, the first character is written in **Inverted-V Path**. A part is added to the **top, left or bottom** side of the first character. Colour the second character in the correct Part Order using the Part Order Colour Code.

Inverted-V + Part

Left + Inverted-V

Top + Inverted-V

Inverted-V + Bottom

Part Order
1 2 3 4 5

Activity 50

These characters are like **Quartets** (following the Inverted-N Path) or like **L2R Complex** (in columns). Colour the characters in the correct Part Order according to the Part Order Colour Code.

Part Order
1 2 3 4 5 6

Activity 51

These characters has three columns. Write from **left to right (L2R)** from the first to second then to third column. Before moving from one column to another, goes down **(T2B)** in each column – following the Inverted-N Path. See example.

Colour the characters in the correct Part Order according to the Part Order Colour Code.

Part Order
1 2 3 4 5 6

Activity 52

In each pair of characters, the first character is a **T2B Triplet** with 3 or more parts. Two alphabets are added to the top of the first character.

Colour the characters in the Part Order according to the Part Order Colour Code.

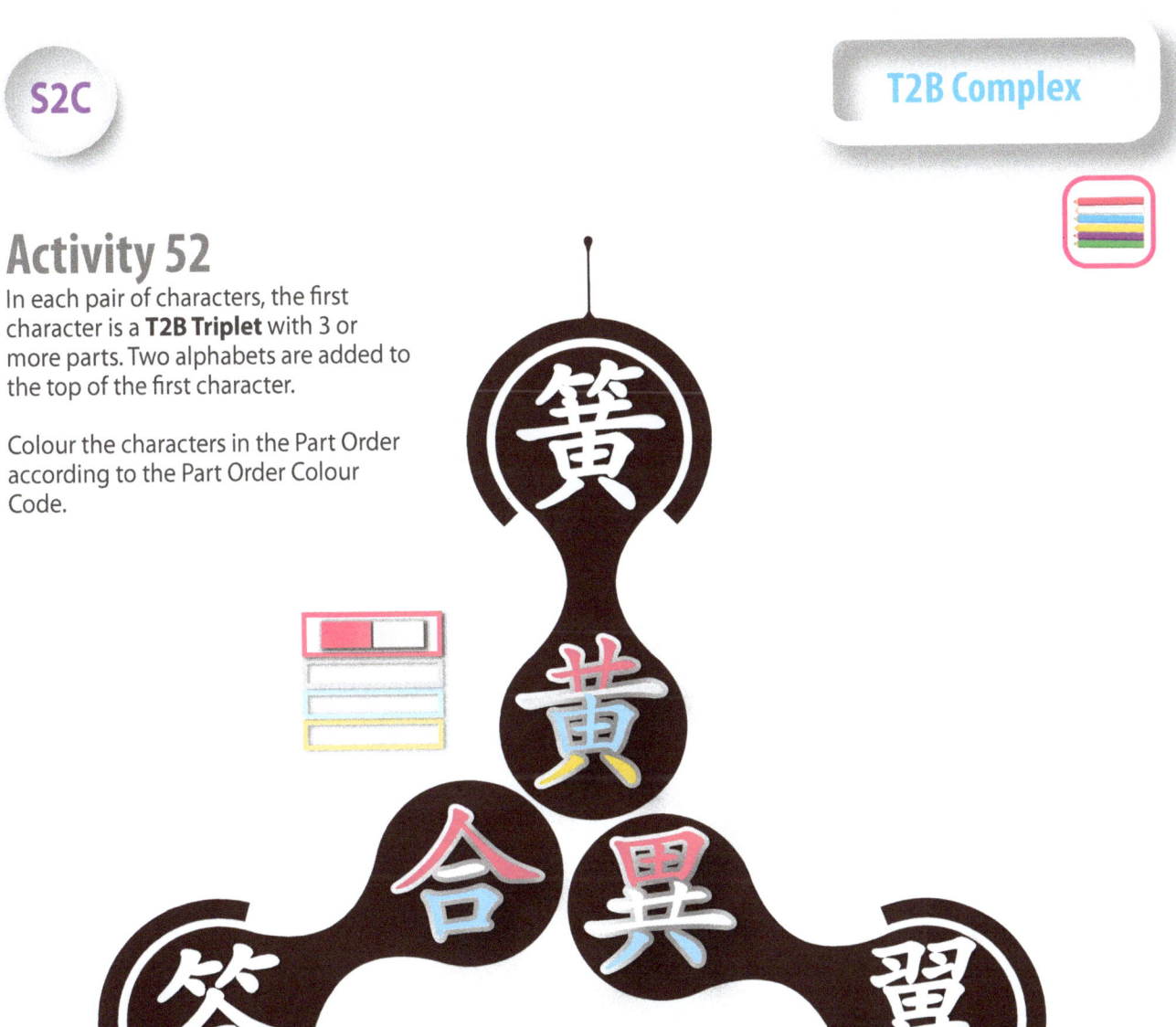

Part Order
1 2 3 4 5 6

Activity 53

These characters are **Acute-L Complex**. Note that the top portion of the characters are made up of **2 parts**.

Colour the characters in the correct Part Order according to the Part Order Colour Code.

Part Order
1 2 3 4

Activity 54

These characters are **Acute-L Complex**. Note that the top portion of the characters are made up of **3 parts**. Colour the characters in the correct Part Order according to the Part Order Colour Code.

Activity 55

These characters are **Acute-7 Complex**. Note the bottom portion of these characters are made up of **2 or 3 parts**. In one character, two parts are added to the top.

Acute-7 Complex

Colour the characters in the correct Part Order according to the Part Order Colour Code.

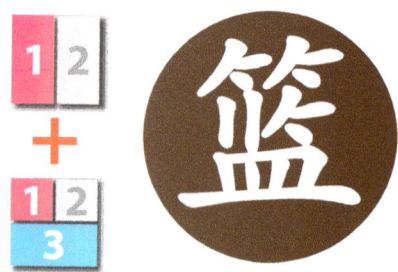

This character is created by combining two standard structures

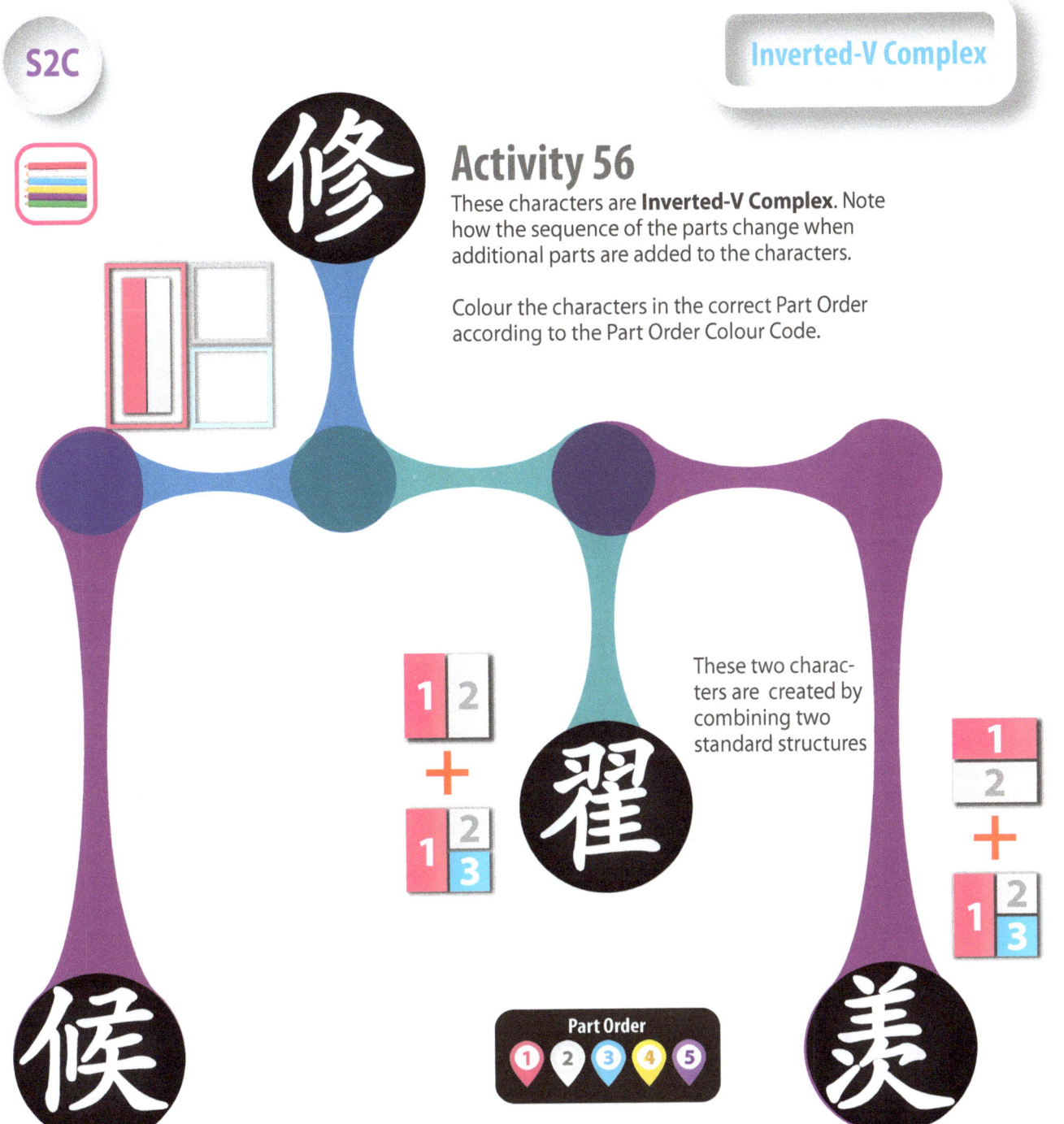

Activity 56

These characters are **Inverted-V Complex**. Note how the sequence of the parts change when additional parts are added to the characters.

Colour the characters in the correct Part Order according to the Part Order Colour Code.

These two characters are created by combining two standard structures

Part Order
1 2 3 4 5

Activity 57

Observe how the characters get more complex when parts are added to the characters at different stages. Colour the characters in the correct Part Order according to the Part Order Colour Code.

至

到
(1) T2R + R

倒
(2) T2B + R + L

百

佰
(1) T2B + L

宿
(2) T2R + L + T

蓿
(3) T2B + L + T + T

品

杲
(1) Acute-L Path + B

澡
(2) Acute-L Path + B + L

藻
(3) Acute-L Path + B + L + T

Part Order
1 2 3 4 5 6

Activity 58

Observe how the characters get more complex when parts are added to the characters at different stages. Colour the characters in the correct Part Order according to the Part Order Colour Code.

S2C

Part Order
① ② ③ ④ ⑤

Activity 59

Observe how the characters get more complex when parts are added to the characters at different stages. Colour the characters in the correct Part Order according to the Part Order Colour Code.

Part Order
1 2 3 4 5

Activity 60

Observe how the characters get more complex when parts are added to the characters at different stages. Colour the characters in the correct Part Order according to the Part Order Colour Code.

Part Order
1 2 3 4 5 6

How to Construct/Decode Complex Characters

The following are the different types of complex characters you have come across in this section. Analyse how characters with complex structures can be constructed from simple structures. This would help you to decode complex characters easily.

Add a Part

Add a part to the left side of a character with T2B structure is represented by this symbol (below left). Observe Part Order of the newly-formed character. More structures are shown below.

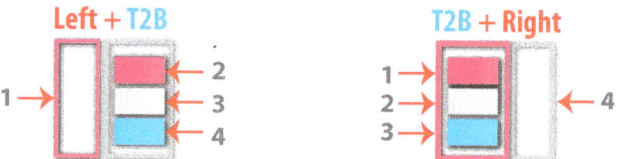

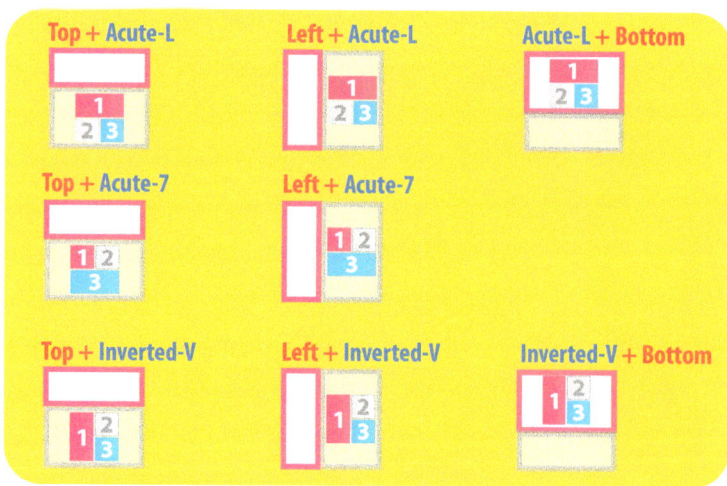

Add Multiple Parts

Add a part one at a time at different stages to make the character more complex.

Embedded

In some characters, one or more structures are embedded into another structure.

L2R Complex

T2B Complex

Acute-L Complex

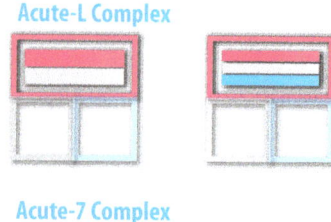

Acute-7 Complex

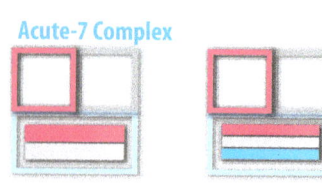

Inverted-V Complex

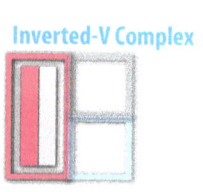

144   **SIMPLE TO COMPLEX**

Activity 61

These characters are created in one or more structures. Match the character to its structure(s) by writing the number(s) in the given box. See example.

1) **L2R Path**

2) **T2B Path**

3) **I4O**: L-Frame

4) **Combi**: Acute-7

5) **Combi**: Inverted-N

6) **Combi**: Z-Path

7) **O4I**: Inverse 7-Frame

8) **O4I**: L-Frame

9) **O4I**: 7-Frame

10) **OIO**: Enclosure

11) **OIO**: 7-Frame

12) **OIO**: Flipped C-Frame

匠		声	2, 11	哥	
勿		赵		易	
盾		派		那	1, 9
卤		疒		筐	

Activity 62

These characters are created in one or more structures. Match the character to its structure(s) by writing the number(s) in the given box. See example.

1) **L2R Path**

2) **T2B Path**

3) **I40: L-Frame**

4) **Combi: Acute-7**

5) **Combi: Inverted-N**

6) **Combi: Z-Path**

7) **O4I: Inverse 7-Frame**

8) **O4I: L-Frame**

9) **O4I: n-Frame**

10) **O4I: 7-Frame**

11) **FPF: Flag Pole First**

12) **FPL: Flag Pole Last**

挺 ☐

辰 ☐

随 ☐

即 ☐

汤 ☐

兕 ☐

局 **7, 12, 10**

改 ☐

包 ☐

抛 ☐

高 ☐

翘 ☐

起 ☐

爬 ☐

屏 ☐

阒 ☐

庶 ☐

刨 ☐

CHARACTERS WITH INTERSECTING PARTS

IPO

Intersecting Part Order

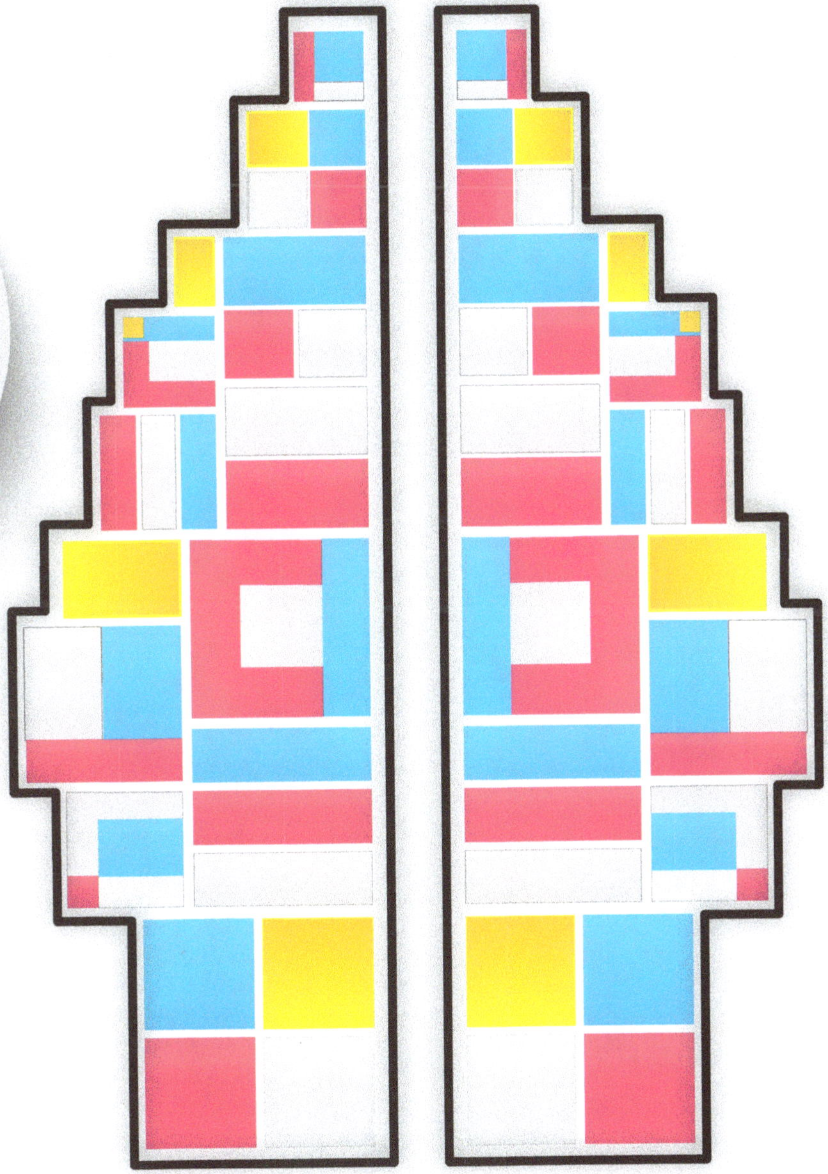

Intersecting **P**arts **O**rder

Horizontal(s) First

Horizontal Last

RL-Slash Intersects

Enclosure (Horizontal)

Enclosure (Empty)

Flipped C-Frame / C-Frame

U-Frame / Horizontal Hook Intersects

n-Frame

Intersecting Dot(s)

In these characters, the top **Horizontal** stroke is written **FIRST**, it is intersected by an alphabet. Take note of the **Cross Point(s)** in the characters.

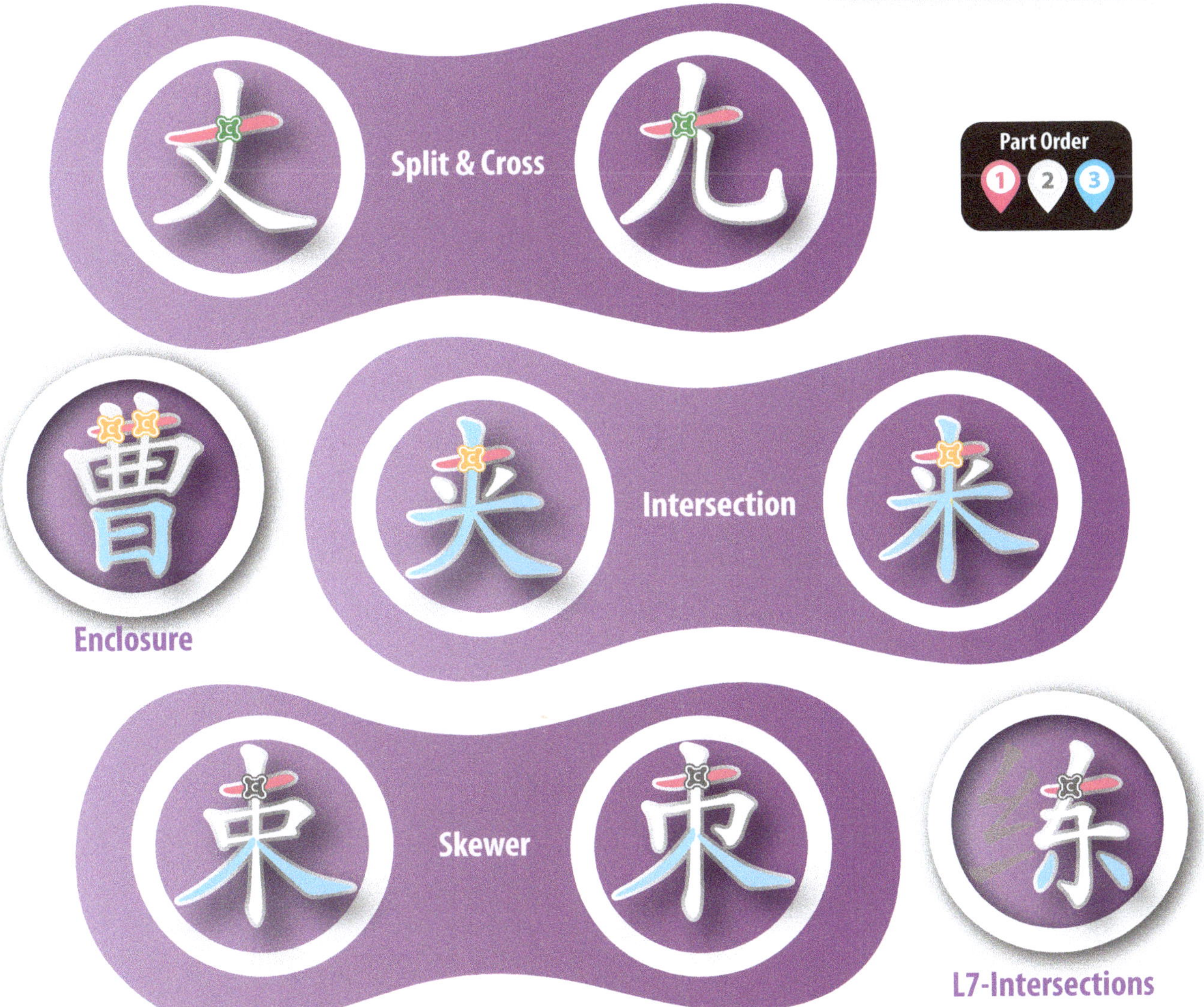

Horizontal First

Split & Cross

文 九

Part Order
① ② ③

曹

Enclosure

头 来

Intersection

束 束 练

Skewer

L7-Intersections

In these characters, the **two Horizontals** are written **FIRST**. They are intersected by an alphabet. Take note of the **Cross Point(s)** in the characters.

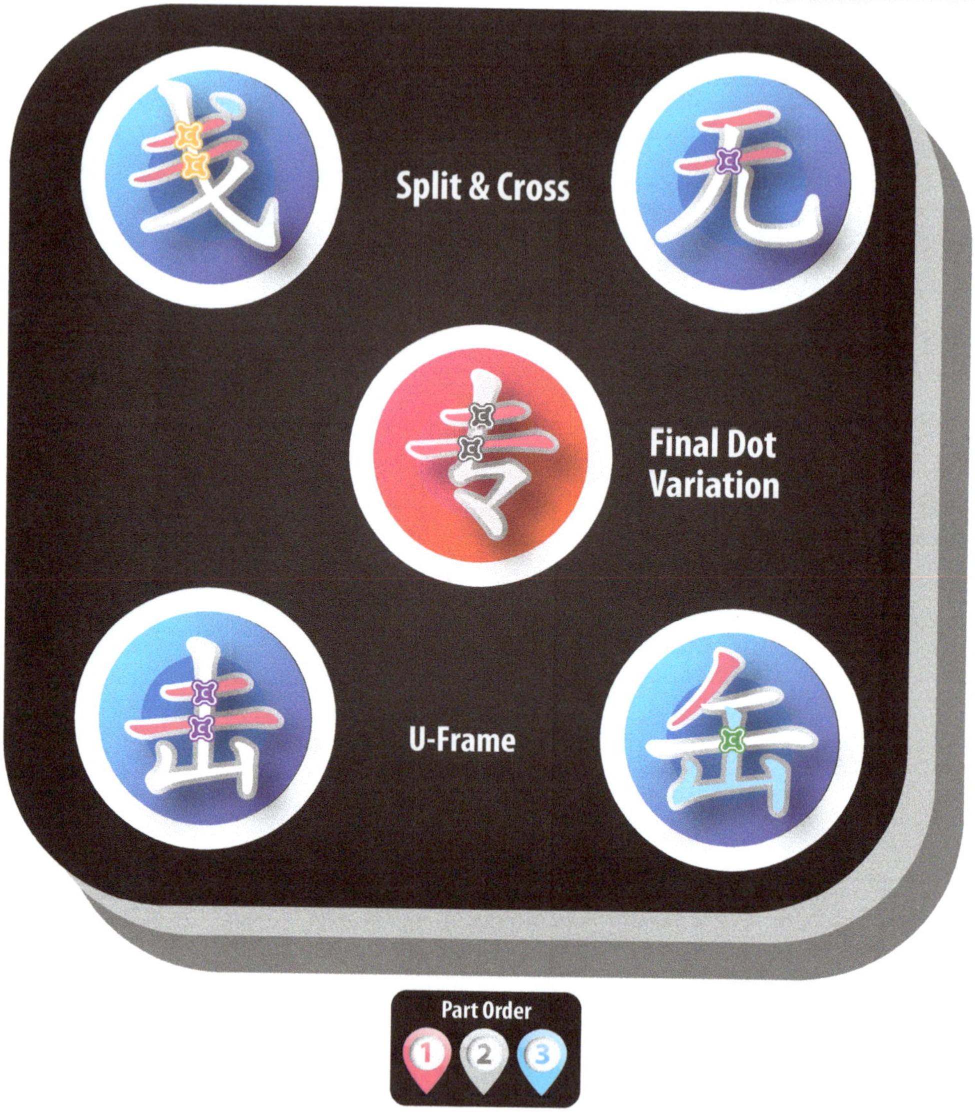

Split & Cross

Final Dot
Variation

U-Frame

Part Order
1 2 3

Contrary to the previous set of characters, the **Horizontal** stroke in these characters is written **LAST**. The Horizontal stroke intersects other alphabet/stroke(s). Take note of the **Cross Point(s)** in the characters.

母

贯

L7-Enclosure

女 Cross (Exception)

本 Intersection

册

丹 n-Frame

Part Order
1 2 3

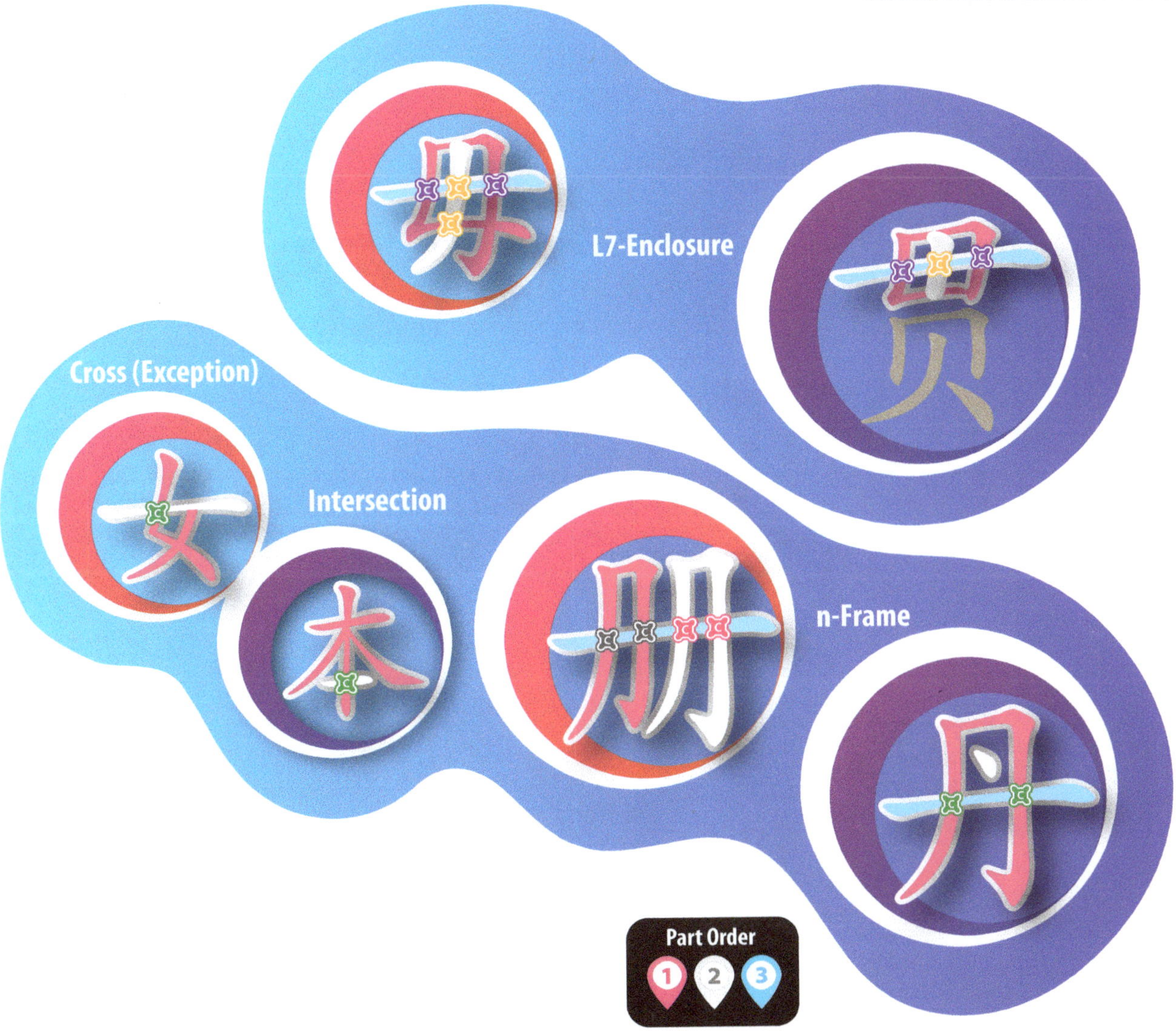

Activity 63

Round up the characters in the given shapes to classify them according to the Part Order of the **outlined parts.** Colour the **outlined parts** in the corect Part Order according to the given colour code.

Horizontal First

Horizontal Last

Part Order
1 2 3

仕　安

彤　沛　奴

笨

要　枣　鱿

爽　删　糟

Activity 64

These characters have intersecting parts. Colour the parts that are not coloured. Indicate the **B**ond Points and **C**ross Points. See examples

Part Order
① ② ③ ④ ⑤ ⑥

陆肺传

菜

委

窑

线

芜练羌

盏英妥

Zoom in on the **RL-Slash** in these characters. The RL-Slash intersects a stroke or alphabet. Take note of the the **C**ross **Point** in the characters.

RL-Slash intersects with Curl-Up or Intersection or Enclosure Variation

Curl-Up

Part Order
1 2 3 4 5

Intersection

RL-Slash–

Enclosure Variation

Recall the alphabet in the qTRAIL **Enclosure (Horizontal)**. It is written **FIRST** in these characters. Observe how another stroke or alphabet intersects with it. Take note of the **Cross Points** in the characters.

Enclosure (Horizontal)

Enclosure (Horizontal) intersects with Vertical or L-Hook

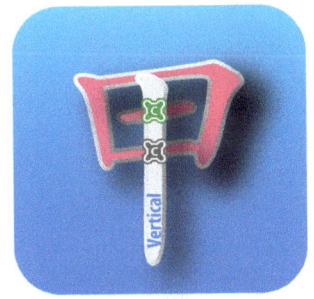
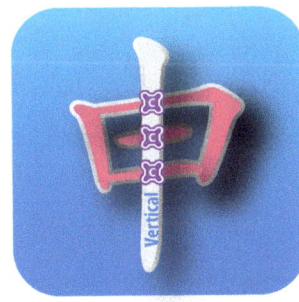
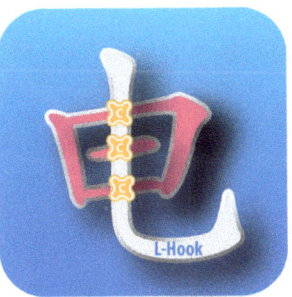

Enclosure (Horizontal) intersects with Intersection / Cross

Recall the alphabet in the qTRAIL **Enclosure (Blank)**. It is written **FIRST** before it is being intersected by another part. Take note of the **C**ross Points in the characters.

Perpendicular

Cross

Skewer

Variations

Intersection

Intersection (Tail Bottom)

Split

Part Order
1 2 3 4

Split

Marching

The alphabet **Flipped C-Frame** is written **FIRST** except for one character. Observe how another part intersects it. Take note of the **C**ross Points in the characters.

Flipped C-Frame written LAST

Part Order
① ② ③

C-Frame

The alphabet **C-Frame** is written **FIRST** in these characters. Observe how another stroke or alphabet intersects with it. Take note of the **C**ross Points in the characters.

The alphabet **U-Frame** is intersected by another stroke or alphabet. Take note of the **Cross Points** in the characters.

Horizontal Hook + ...

These alphabets with **Horizontal Hook** is intersected by another stroke or alphabet. Take note of the **Cross Point** in the characters.

Part Order
1 2 3 4

Activity 65

Observe the characters (in green squares) and distinguish the parts in these characters. For each character, **link up the parts** (in circles) by tracing the dotted lines (using different colours for different colours) from the first part to the last part. See example below. Note some parts are used more than once.

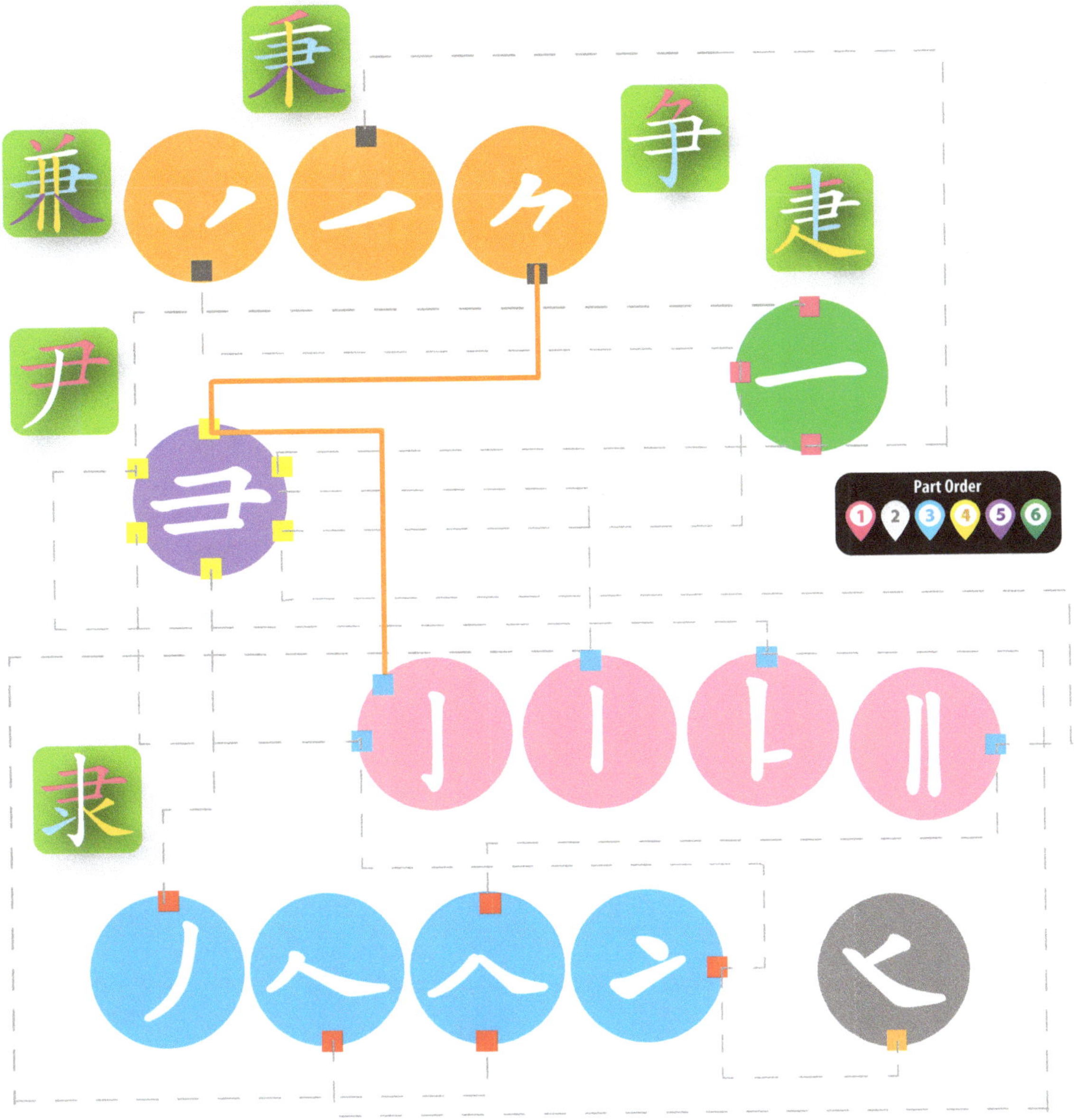

Part Order
① ② ③ ④ ⑤ ⑥

Activity 66

 **IPO**

Observe the characters (in squares) and distinguish the parts in these characters. For each character, **link up the parts** (in circles) by drawing lines (using different colours for different colours) from the first part to the last part. See example below. Note some parts are used more than once.

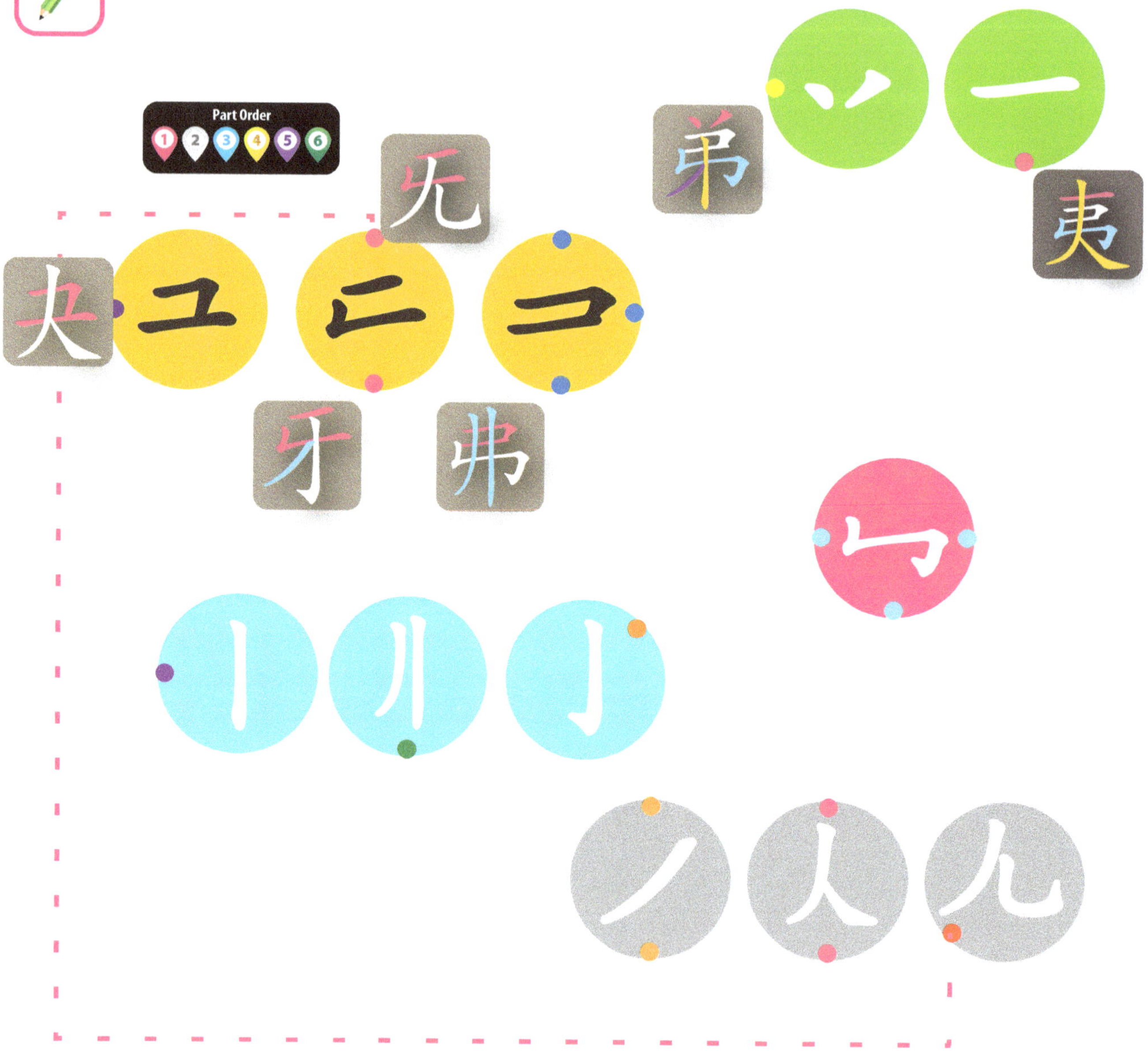

Part Order
1 2 3 4 5 6

The alphabet **n-Frame** is written **FIRST** in these characters. Observe how another part intersects it. Take note of the **Cross Points** in the characters.

n-Frame

Part Order
1 2 3 4 5 6

内 冉

西 甫 庸

离 禺 禺

Intersects 2 parts

Activity 67

Put a tick in the box that shows the correct Part Order of the character. Colour the parts in the correct Part Order according to the colour code given. See example.

课
- ✓ 〕日 木
- ☐ 〕田 木

匣
- ☐ 一 叵 儿
- ☐ 一 田 儿

建
- ☐ 肀 聿 廴
- ☐ 肀 聿 廴

蜣
- ☐ 叶 亠 王 儿
- ☐ 叶 亠 三 儿

陆
- ☐ 阝 二 山
- ☐ 阝 土 山

屈
- ☐ 𡉄 丿 中 凵
- ☐ 𡉄 丿 山 凵

量
- ☐ 日 一 日 土
- ☐ 日 一 田 土

使
- ☐ 亻 十 口 乂
- ☐ 亻 一 口 乂

妾
- ☐ 丶 亠 丷 一 女 一
- ☐ 丶 亠 丷 一 一 女

馋
- ☐ 𠂆 𠃌 口 儿 冫
- ☐ 𠂆 𠃌 口 四 儿 冫

Activity 68

Put a tick in the box that shows the correct Part Order of the character. Colour the parts in the correct Part Order according to the colour code given.

Part Order ① ② ③ ④ ⑤ ⑥

耦
- [ ] 耒 日 冂 小
- [ ] 耒 田 冂 小

軟
- [ ] 一 中 人 厶 人
- [ ] 十 四 人 厶 人

象
- [ ] 々 口 豕 乀
- [ ] 々 四 豕 乀

棘
- [ ] 中 一 人 中 一 人
- [ ] 一 中 人 一 中 人

逆
- [ ] 丷 一 屮 辶
- [ ] 丷 一 屮 丿 辶

專
- [ ] 一 口 龶 寸 丶
- [ ] 十 用 龶 寸 丶

重
- [ ] 一 十 田 土
- [ ] 一 一 曰 土

魅
- [ ] 丿 曰 儿 厶 未
- [ ] 丿 田 儿 厶 未

禹
- [ ] 一 口 冂 小
- [ ] 一 中 冂 小

妻
- [ ] 十 彐 女 一
- [ ] 一 彐 女 一

In the standard part order rules DOF (Dots First) and DOL (Dots Last), the dots do not intersect other strokes. When a dot intersects a stroke, the dot(s) is written after that alphabet/stroke.

Part Order
1 2 3 4 5

斤

九

匆

奈

Colour the parts in the character in the correct Part Order according to the colour code given. Indicate the **Bond Points** and **Cross Points** of the **parts**.

Part Order
1 2 3 4 5 6

龟　策　宴

再　波　军

身　缸　更

农　西　老

✓

夕日乚

一刀土

㇇㇒十

丶刂丿

丶亻弋

丶宀日攵一

竹一巾人

氵厂丨又

丿二山工

一日乂

土丿匕

一冂儿二

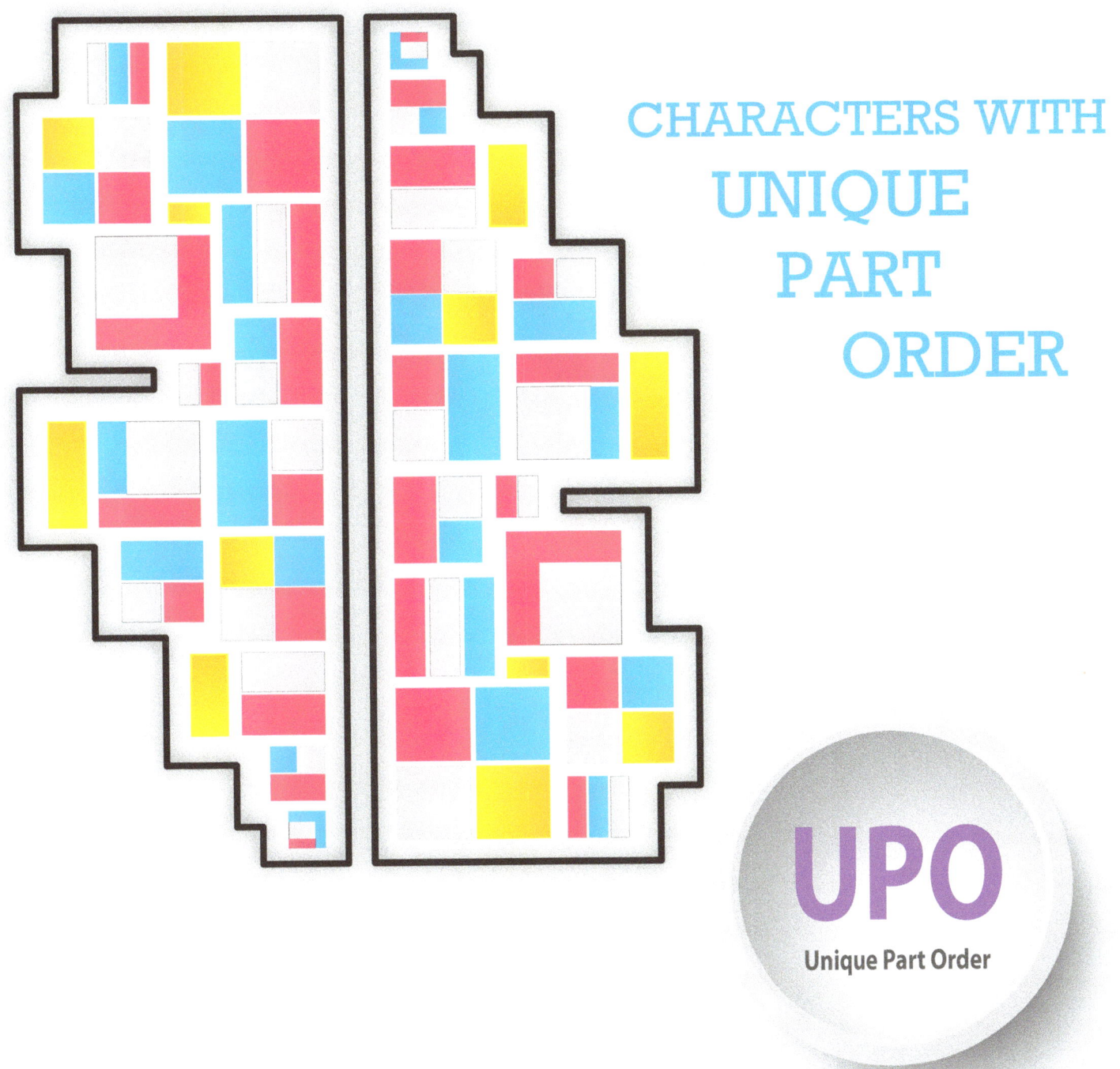

CHARACTERS WITH
UNIQUE
PART
ORDER

UPO
Unique Part Order

Unique Part Order

Clockwise

Alternate Dot(s)

Middle or Sides

With L-Bend or L7-Bends

Bonded / Apart

Crossed

Start from the leftmost **Vertical** and moves to the stroke on the right of it until the bottom **Horizontal**. Note these two strokes **7L-Bends** and **Double-7 Bends** appear in these characters and not in other characters. Are you able to identify them?

Start from leftmost Vertical

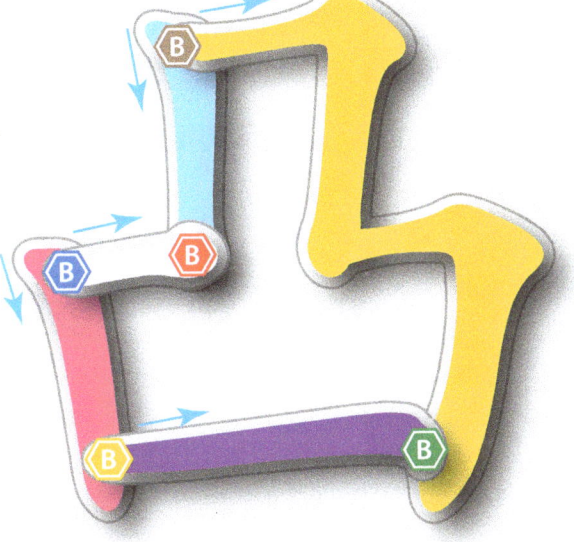

7L-Bends

Double-7 Bends

In these characters, dots are written in-between other strokes from left to right or top to bottom.

Alternate Dot(s)

 **A** **From Left to Right**

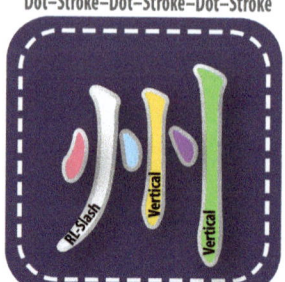

Dot–Stroke–Dot–Stroke–Dot–Stroke

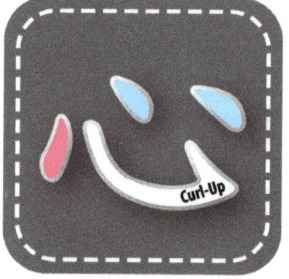

Part Order
① 1 ② 2 ③ 3 ④ 4 ⑤ 5 ⑥ 6

B **From Top to Bottom**

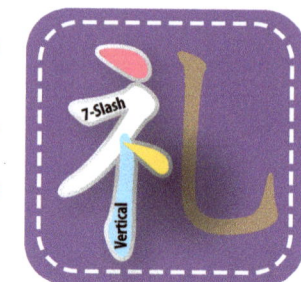

 **C** **Frame >> Dot >> Horizontal >> Dot (if any)**

In these characters, the outer parts (e.g. **n-frame** or **L7-Intersection**) is wrritten first, followed by **Dot, Horizontal and Dot** (if any).

Variation

170   **UNIQUE PART ORDER**

 **Middle Left >> Left >> Middle Right >> Right**

Stroke –Dots (Tick)–Stroke–Dots

Take note whether the strokes on the sides or in the middle are written first in each of these characters.

Compare this character with those that follow the **M4S and S4M** rules.

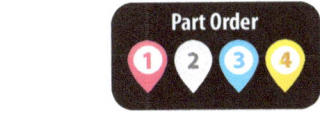

 **Sides >> Middle**

 **Middle >> Sides >> Middle Left >> Middle Right**

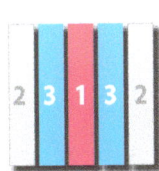

G Flag (L-Bend)

H L7-Bends

Perpendicular
Variation

I Perpendicular Variaton +
L-Bend

Observe the parts coloured in
the Part Order Colour Codes.
They look very similar because

- They share a common part
  * *Perpendicular Variation*

- They have similar parts
  * *Flag (L-Bend) alphabet*
  * *L7-Bends stroke*
  * *L-Bend stroke*

Compare and distinguish them.

Observe how the parts bond to one another. These characters have unique composition that are not usually seen in other characters.

 Bonded

 **Bonded**

Note down your own observations

Rarely does the 1st stroke of a character start from the top-right corner

This one does!

Another rare sight

Observe how the parts are attached to an almost-vertical RL-Slash

Unique selection of components and unique combination of these components

See what is inside the enclosure

This is an unique way to create an enclosure for the dot

Note down your own observations

This character has some resemblance to simpler characters but it is much more complex in its composition

Note how all the parts are bonded to one another

Compare with this character:

An extension of the previous character

Imagine poking something into a container

K Apart

Look at the upper portion of the character

Many learners thought the two horizontals are bonded to the n-Frame

They are NOT!!

You probably remember seeing a couple of characters with the L7-Hook alphabet and Horizontal

This character is unique as the horizontal is replaced by four dots

Compare the upper portion with this character:

Crossed

Observe how the parts cross one another. These characters are unique in the way the parts cross one another. Bond Points (BPs) are not shown here to help you focus just on the Cross Points (CPs).

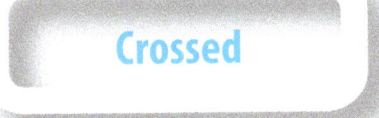

Crossed

Part Order
1 2 3 4

Note down your own observations

Recall the Stroke Order of the first part

Contrary to the usual stroke order, the Vertical is written before the top Horizontal

The RL-Slash intersecting the Enclosure is easily mistaken to be a Vertical

Recall another character which also has a RL-Slash that slashes across the Enclosure

Clue: Look it up in the Intersecting Parts section

Compare with this character:

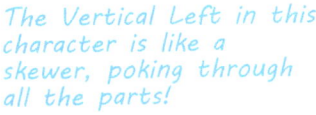

The Vertical Left in this character is like a skewer, poking through all the parts!

Another unique way to create an enclosure by bonding and crossing these parts

Learn Chinese *without* WRITING 3 175

This character will look like a pile of
sticks if decoded stroke by stroke
Its structure is easier to remember if
it is decoded by parts

These two characters are easier to decipher
when the top portion is analysed separately.

The first two parts of these characters are the same
The 3rd part intersects the previous part(s)
One character has 1 CP, the other has 2 CPs

NO Rules. Just Observe!

In this section, you can see that it is not easy to provide a simple rule to describe the Part Order of characters. They may have some resemblance of characters you have seen in earlier sections but they have some peculiarities that make them not conform to conventional rules. Hence, the best way to learn them is not to describe them but just observe them in **colours**.

The following methods will help you to register their images of characters in your mind better.

Write in Your Mind

Visualisation is a good way to remember these characters. Write each character in your mind, part by part. Say 'pink' and imagine the first part of the character appearing, then say 'white' and the second part appears ...

Apart, Bonding, Crossing

Look out for the Bond Points and Cross Points and how far Apart the strokes are positioned.

Alphabets and their Stroke Order

Identify the alphabets in the characters and recall their Stroke Order. Look up in the qTRAILS Map (pages 206 - 209) to confirm that your memory is correct.

Deconstruct & Construct

Take the parts apart and put them together again. This is what you will do in the coming pages. Enjoy!

Activity 70

On the next few pages, characters with Intersecting Parts or Unique Part Order are shown with missing parts. Cut out the missing parts on page 229 and paste them into these characters. The following clues are given to help you solve the puzzles.

1. **Parts are coloured using the Part Order Colour Code**

2. **Bond Point and Cross Point symbols are in different colours**

3. **The first few parts are shown to help you visualise the possible characters**

4. **Partial outlines of some missing parts are also shown**

Paste cut-out strokes onto the correct characters. Align the Bond Point and Cross Point symbols on the strokes and check that the colours are correct. Partial outlines of some of the missing parts are shown.

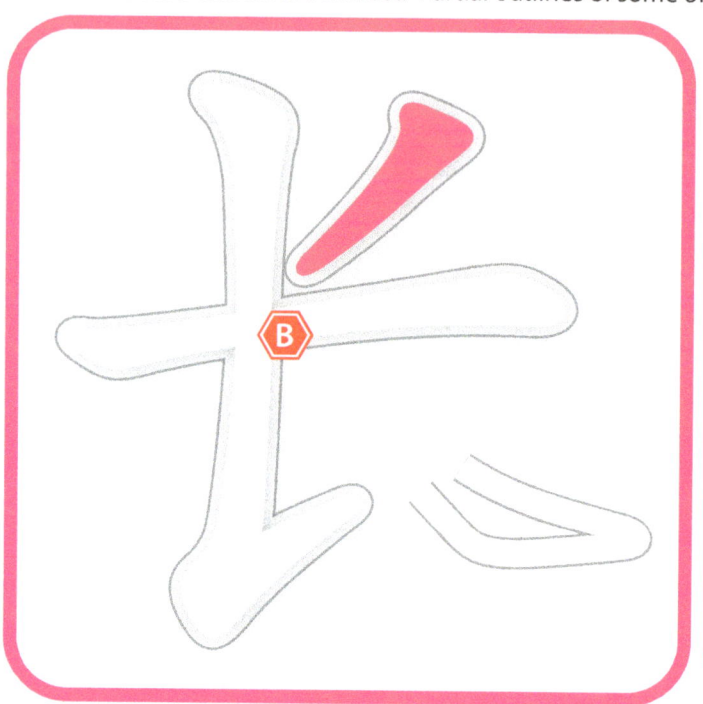

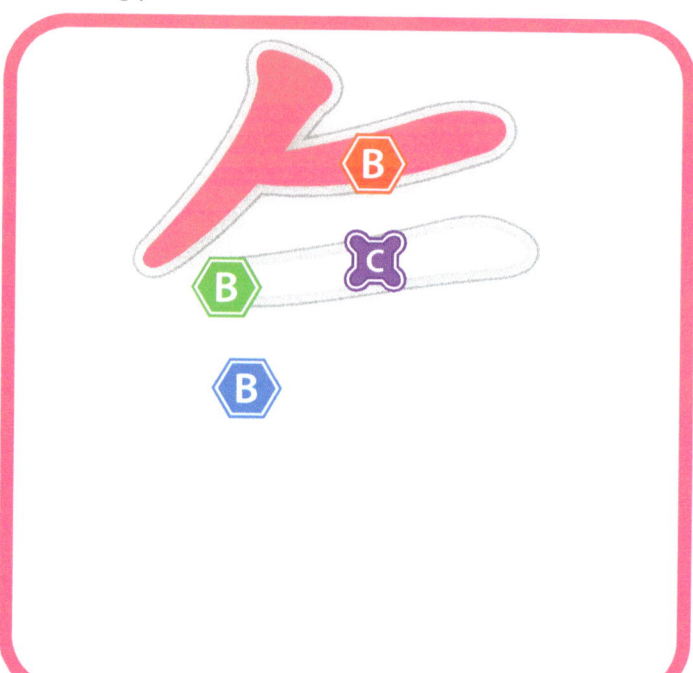

IPO

UPO

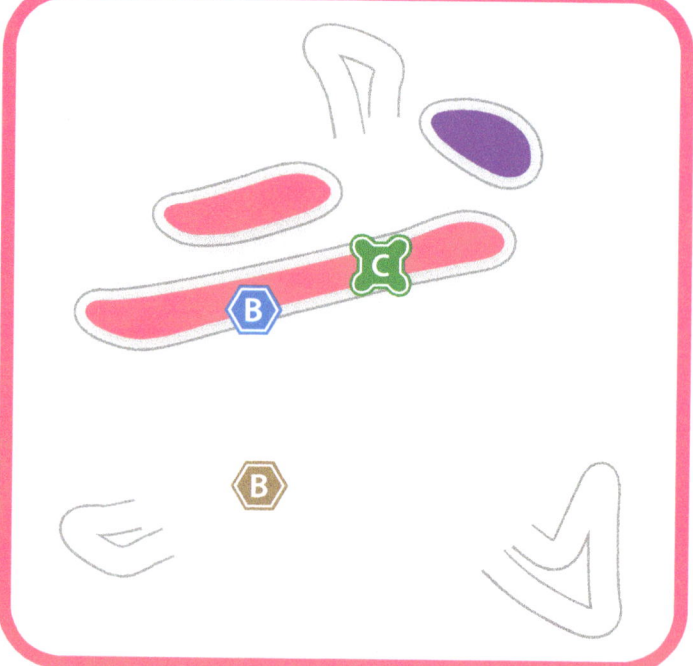

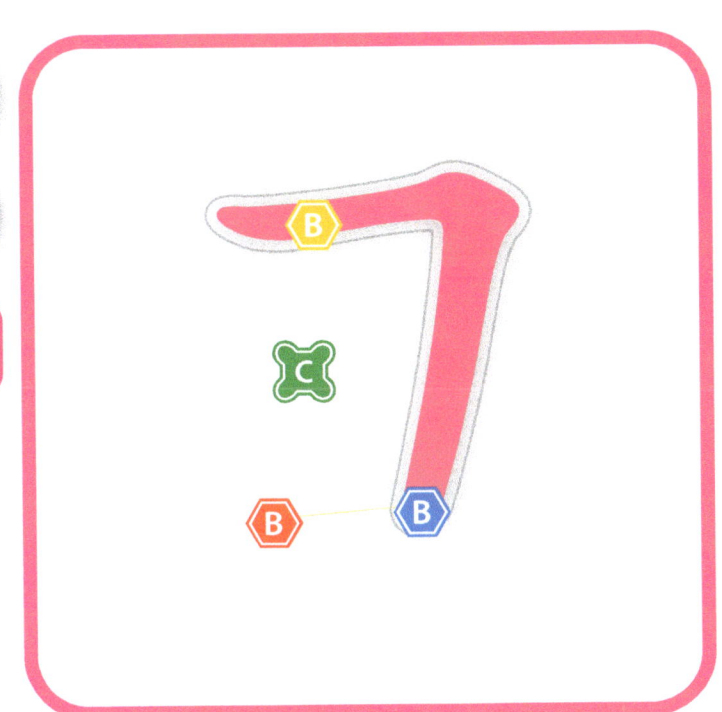

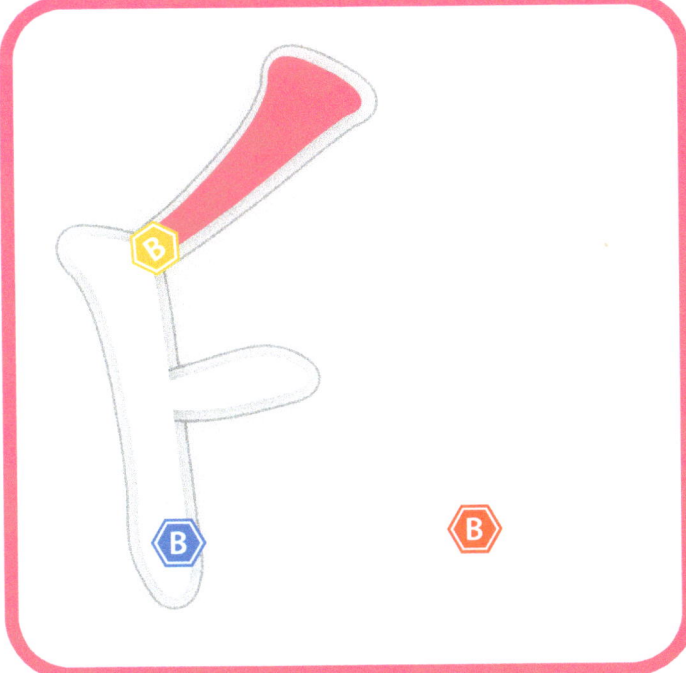

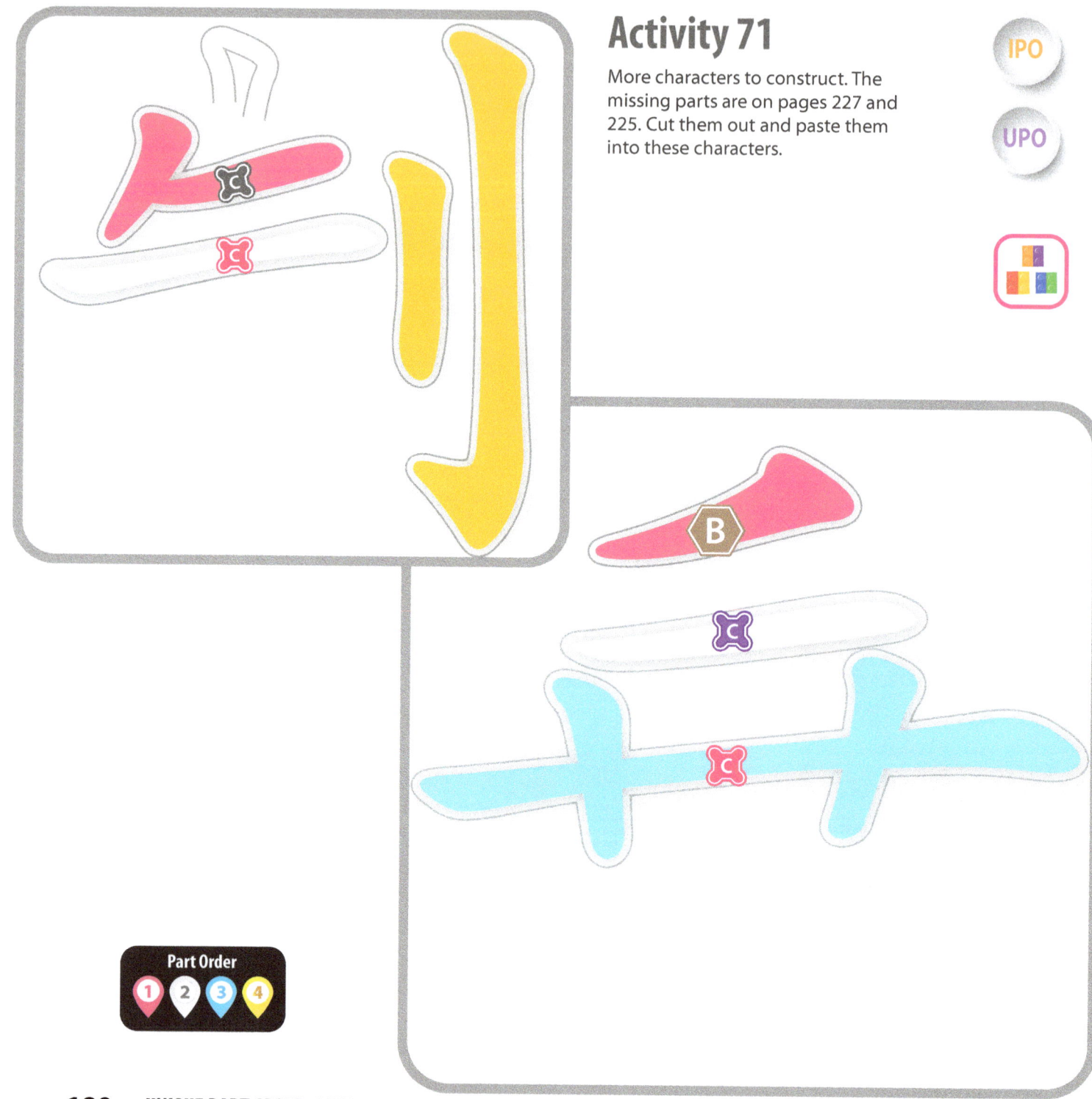

Activity 71

More characters to construct. The missing parts are on pages 227 and 225. Cut them out and paste them into these characters.

IPO

UPO

Part Order
1 2 3 4

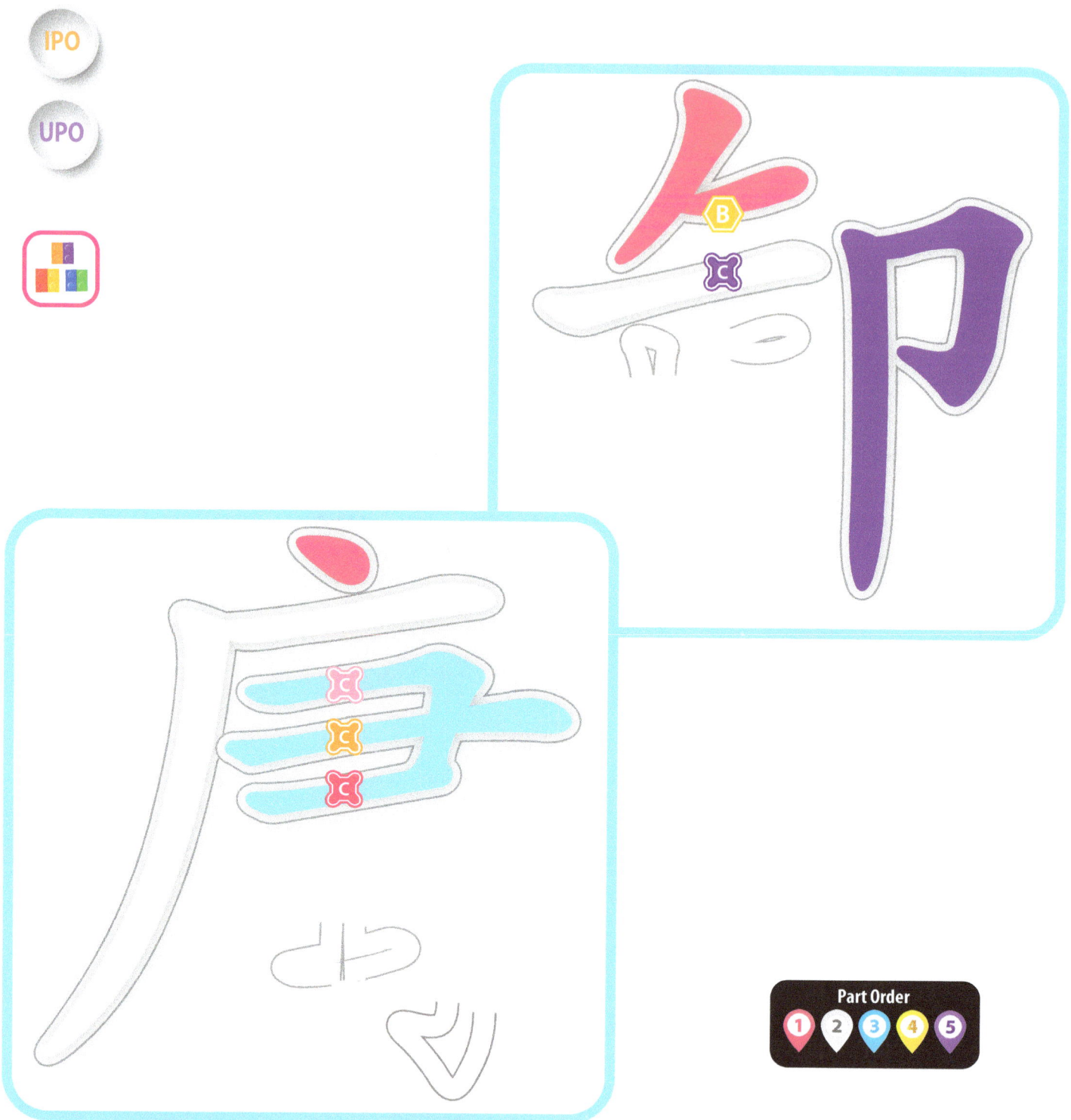

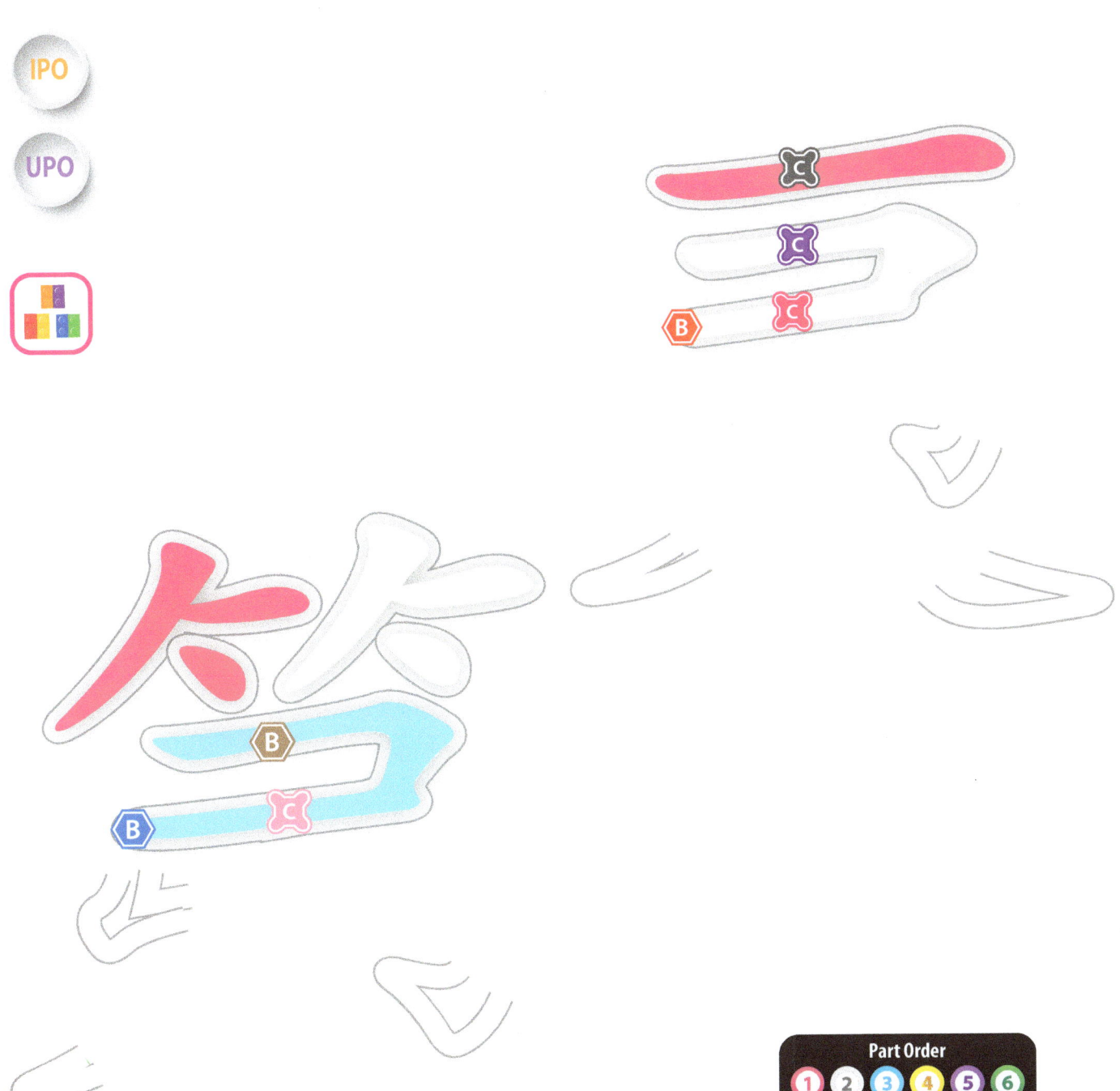

IPO

UPO

L7-Bends

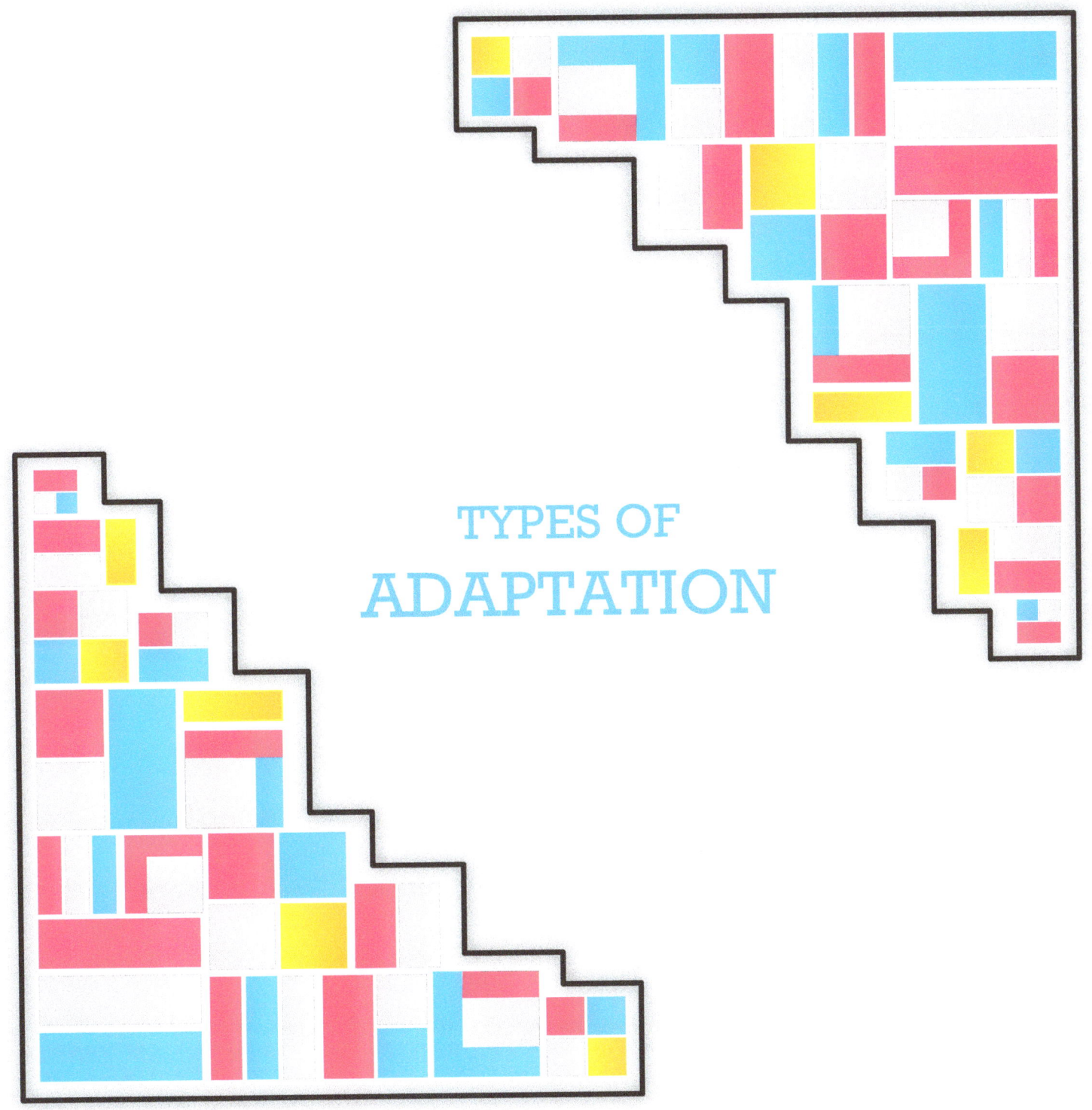

TYPES OF
ADAPTATION

ADAPTATION

In LCWW1, we discussed how parts (alphabets or strokes) adapt themselves so as to fit into characters. See below on the types of adaptations discussed in previous books. In the next few pages, you will see more types of adaptations. Add on other ways of adaptating you observe in the lists below.

(A) SIZE ADAPTATION

1. Flatten

2. Slim down

3. Shrink

4. _____

5. _____

6. _____

(B) STROKE ADAPTATION

1. Change length

2. Slant at different angle

3. Transform into another stroke

4. _____

5. _____

6. _____

Single Adaptation

In LCWW1, Size Adaptation and Stroke Adaptation were discussed separately to make them simpler to understand. Here are some examples of single adaptation.

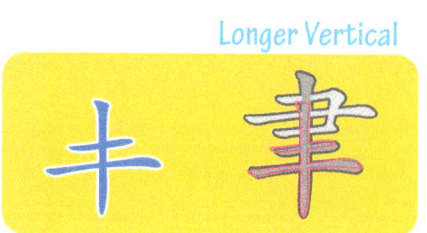

Longer Vertical

Longer RL-Slash

Shrinks

MULTIPLE ADAPTATIONS

In many instances, multiple adaptations are made within characters. Develop the ability to look for such adaptations. Here are some examples.

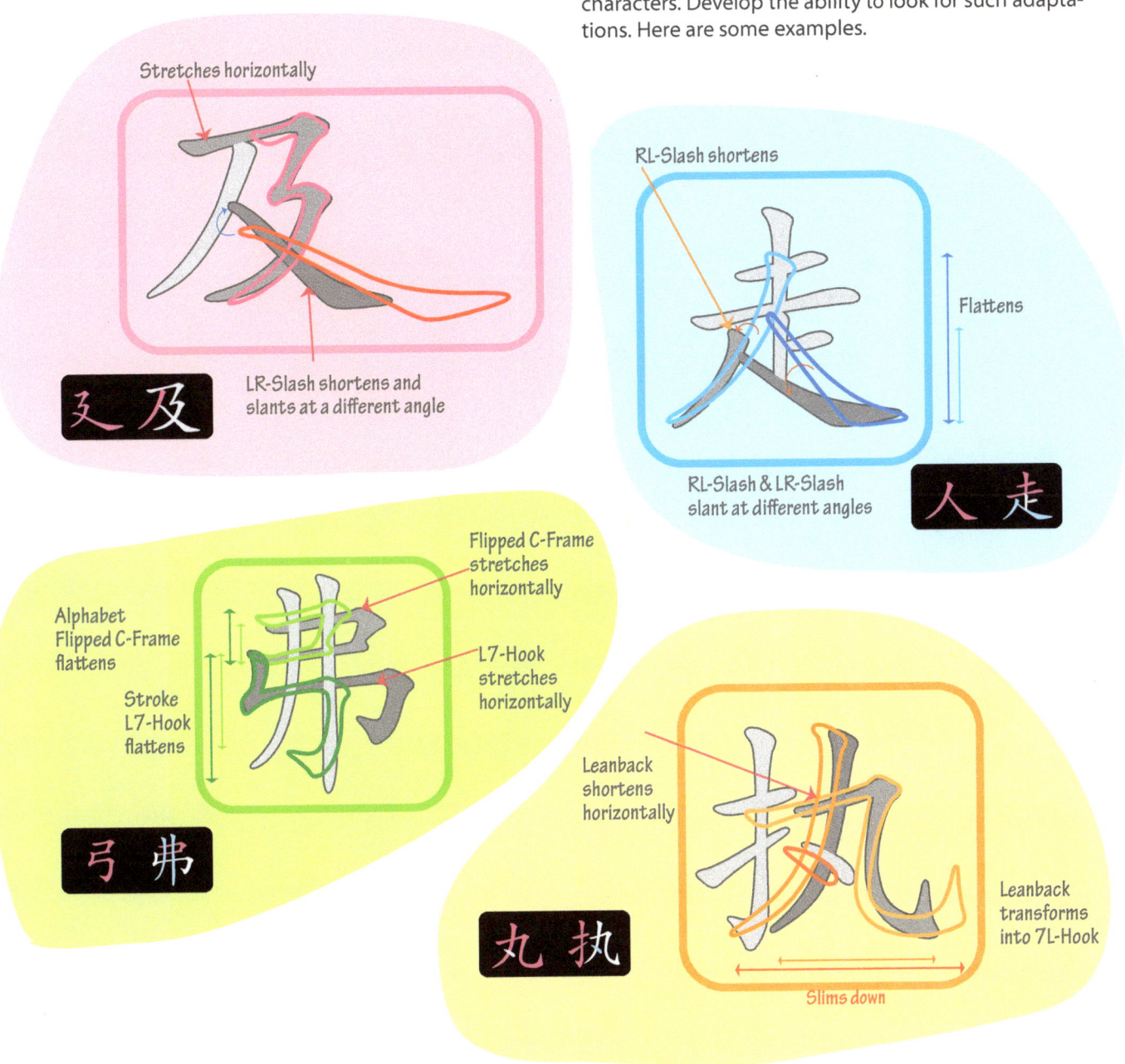

Stretches horizontally

LR-Slash shortens and slants at a different angle

又 及

RL-Slash shortens

Flattens

RL-Slash & LR-Slash slant at different angles

人 走

Alphabet Flipped C-Frame flattens

Flipped C-Frame stretches horizontally

L7-Hook stretches horizontally

Stroke L7-Hook flattens

弓 弗

Leanback shortens horizontally

Leanback transforms into 7L-Hook

Slims down

丸 执

Changes in Strokes ...

Make your own notes on your observations

Stretches →

Slant at different angle

乂

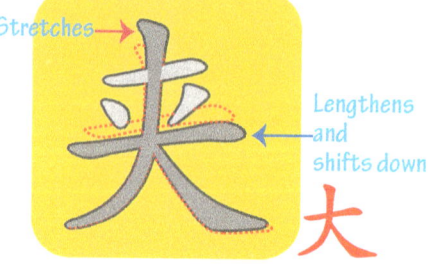

Stretches →

Lengthens and shifts down ←

大

木

串

中

出

山

Slims down / Widens ...

Shorten

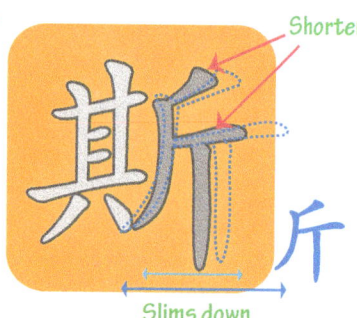

斤

Slims down

Stretches →

Tilt at different angle

人

Slims down

旭

九

勉

免

毯

毛

Widens

Shorten

Expands

雨

巾

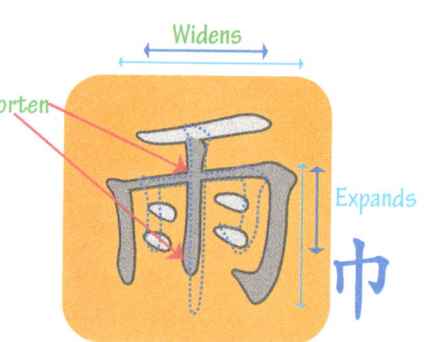

Flattens ...

Make your own notes on your observations

工

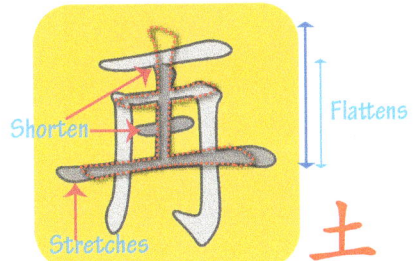

土

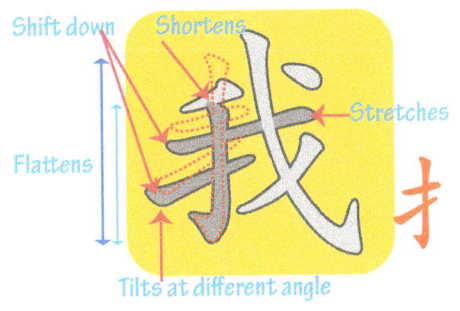

才

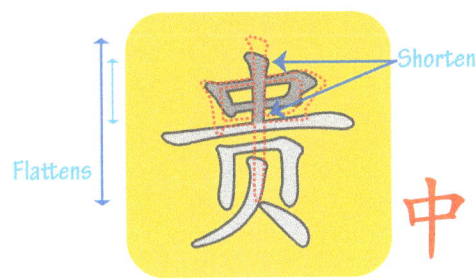

中

Shrinks ...

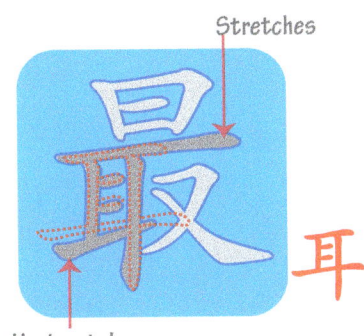

耳

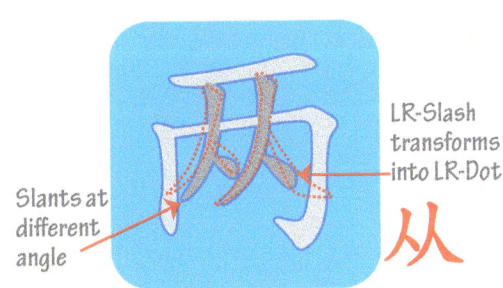

从

士

又

山

木

Adaptation vs Variation

In LCWW2, you learnt that a basic qTRAILS Alphabet can have many *Variations* by making slight changes to it. In this book, you learnt more about *Adaptation*. As both concepts are explained using similar terminologies, there could be some confusion. Now, let's compare the similarities and differences between them.

Adaptation is a process of making changes to parts (alphabets or strokes) so that they can fit into a character

Variations are alphabets created after making changes to the stroke(s) in basic qTRAILS alphabets or other Variations

Below are the differences between Adaptation and Variation:

Changes in Alphabet	Adaptation		Variation	
				Change in size and tilting of strokes at different angles are NOT variations.
1. Change in size	✔	力 架	✘	
2. Change in angle to horizontal of a stroke	✔	叟	✘	
				Basic Alphabet — **Variation**
3. Subtract a stroke	✘	There should NOT be any change in the number of strokes or the structures of characters	✔	三 — 二
4. Add a stroke	✘		✔	了 — 子
5. Convert a Bond Point into Cross Points	✘	There should NOT be any change in the structures of characters	✔	日 — 哀
6. Change relative lengths of strokes	✔	及	✔	土 — 士
7. Change distance between strokes	✔	再	✔	儿 — 见
8. Transform a stroke into another stroke	✔	火 烦	✔	刀 — 乃
9. Change position of a stroke	✔	夹	✔	其 — 耳
10. Change length of one stroke	✔	农	✔	扫 — 录
11. Change the order of strokes	✘		✘	

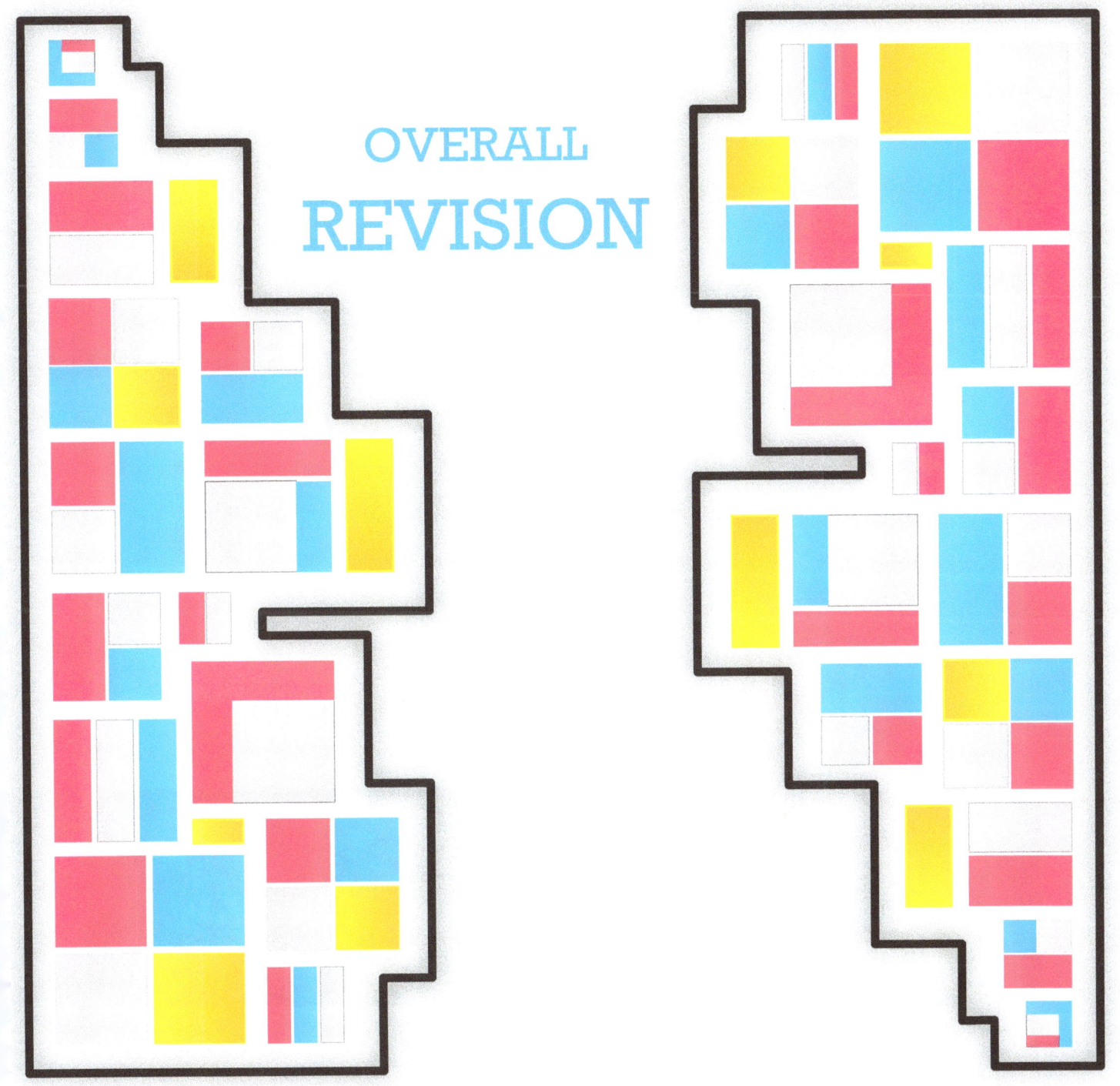

OVERALL
REVISION

Activity 72

Connect the parts of each character by drawing arrows from its first part (indicated with a star) to its last part. Use different coloured arrows for different characters. The first character is done. Some parts are used more than once.

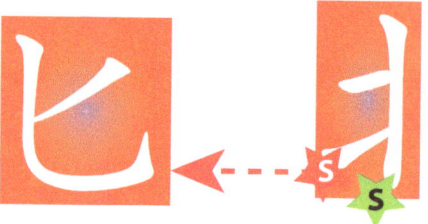

Part Order
1 2 3 4 5 6

Activity 73

Connect the parts of each character by drawing arrows from its first part (indicated with a star) to its last part. Use different coloured arrows for different characters. Some parts are used more than once.

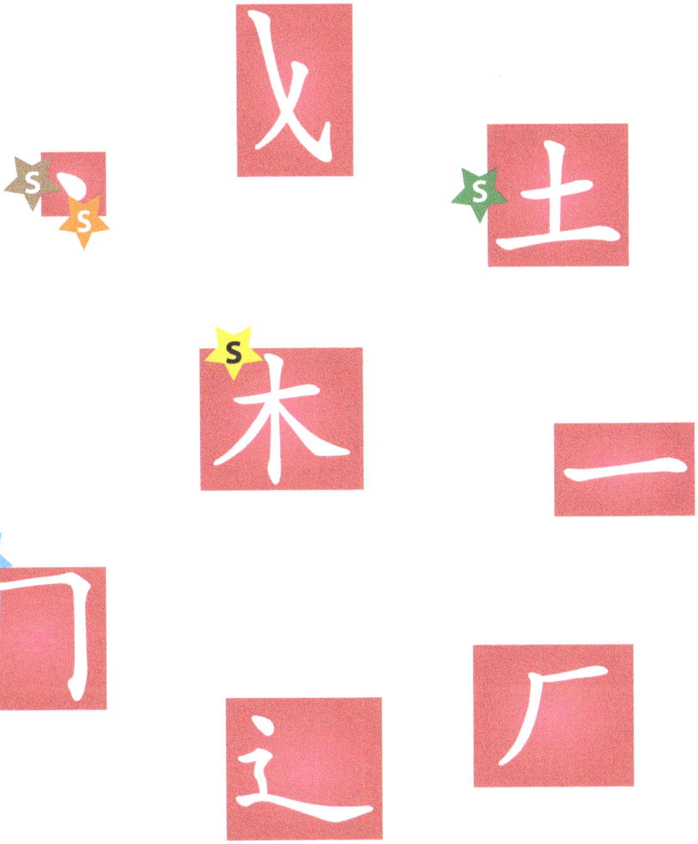
乂
S 丶 S
S 土
门
S 木
一
S 冂
厂
辶

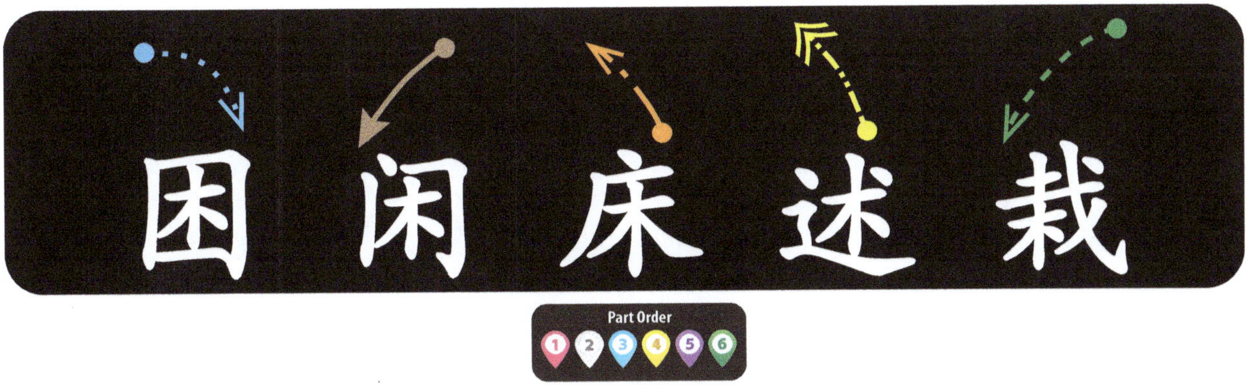
困 闲 床 述 裁
Part Order
1 2 3 4 5 6

Activity 74

Connect the parts of each character by drawing arrows from its first part (indicated with a star) to its last part. Use different coloured arrows for different characters. Some parts are used more than once.

Activity 75

Connect the parts of each character by drawing arrows from its first part (indicated with a star) to its last part. Use different coloured arrows for different characters. Some parts are used more than once.

臧　　鼎　　寐

Part Order
1 2 3 4 5 6

Activity 76

Write the numbers of the parts in the box under the character to show the Part Order of the character.

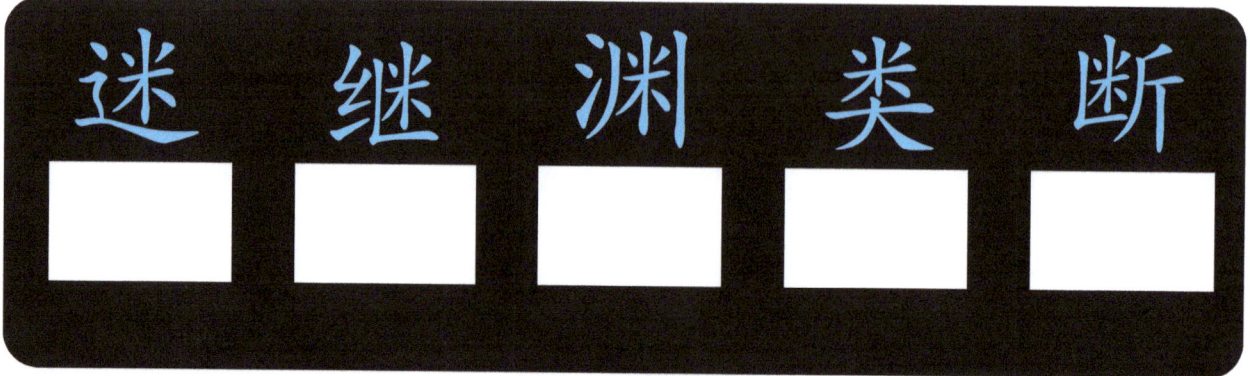

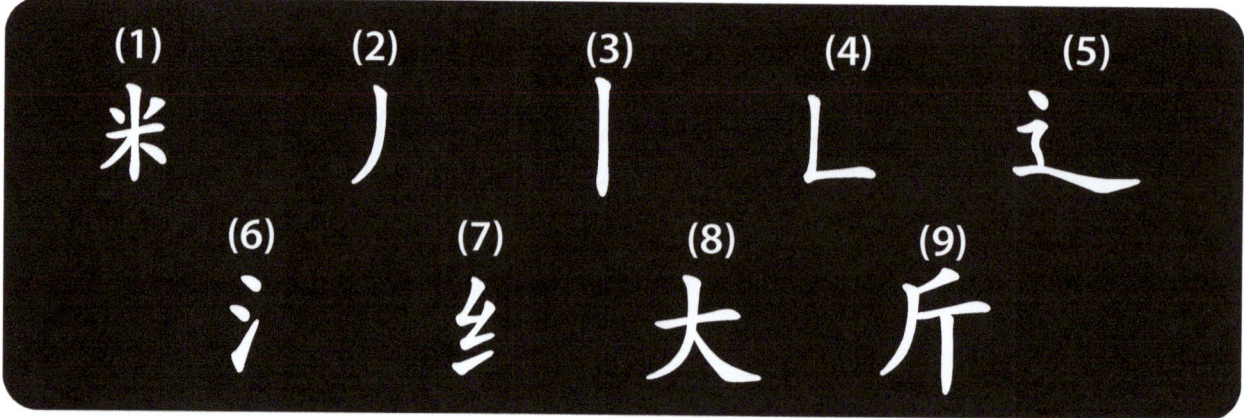

Activity 77

Write the numbers of the parts in the box under the character to show the Part Order of the character.

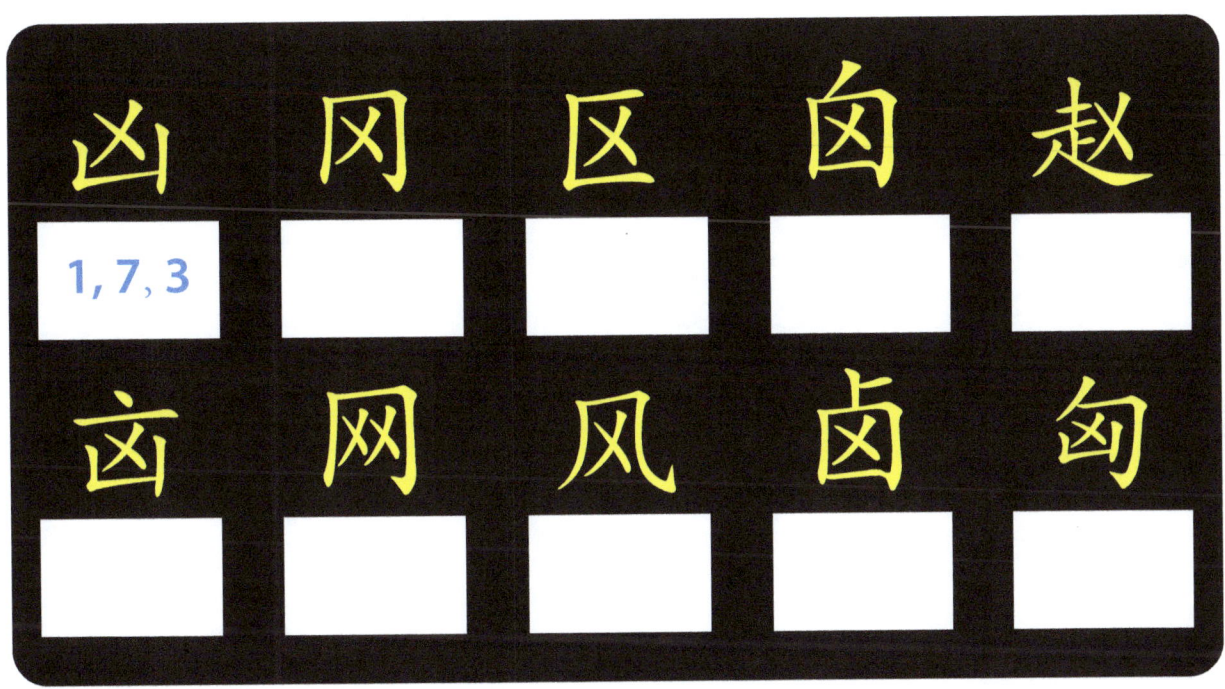

凶 — 1, 7, 3

冈

区

卤

赵

函

网

风

卤

匈

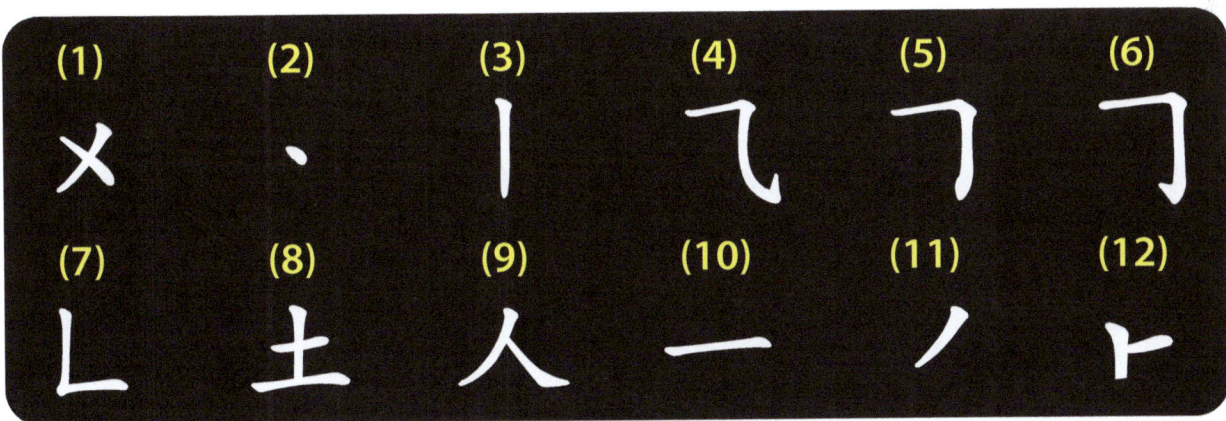

(1)	(2)	(3)	(4)	(5)	(6)
メ	、	丨	乀	乛	勹
(7)	(8)	(9)	(10)	(11)	(12)
ㄴ	土	人	一	丿	⺊

Activity 78 Write the numbers of the parts in the box under the character to show the Part Order of the character.

可　匠　问　司　同

[ ]　[ ]　[ ]　[ ]　[ ]

臣　高　句　回　石

[ ]　[ ]　[ ]　[ ]　[ ]

向　哥　问　同

[ ]　[ ]　[ ]　[ ]

(1)　(2)　(3)　(4)　(5)　(6)　(7)　(8)　(9)　(10)　(11)

口　丶　丿　丨　一　几　乚　𠃌　丿　冂　丁

Activity 79

Write the numbers of the parts in the box under the character to show the Part Order of the character.

户	民	所	段

启	局	官	卤

卢	巴	巨	臣

(1)	(2)	(3)	(4)	(5)	(6)	(7)	(8)	(9)
コ	ノ	l	一	丶	口	㇄	㇆	厂

(10)	(11)	(12)	(13)	(14)	(15)	(16)	(17)	(18)
冂	㇓	丁	又	乜	乚	㇀	㇄	卜

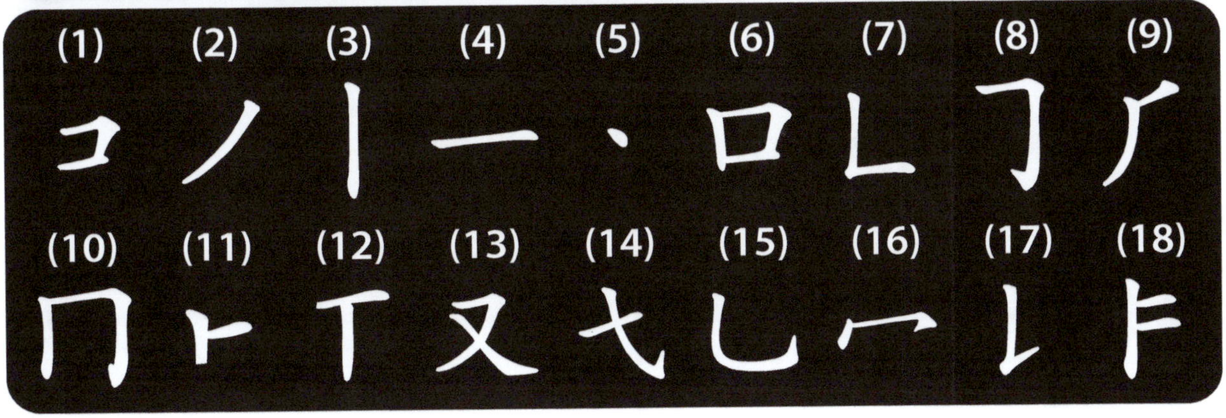

Activity 80

Connect the parts of each character by drawing arrows from its first part to its last part. Note some parts are used more than once. Use different coloured arrows for different characters. See examples.

丿	十	口	广
土	扌	廿	上
厶	匕	匕	灬
月	止	二	人
儿	厶	一	彡

熊　能
庶　燕
背　北
育　肯
些　此
庞　比
乘　乖
舌　古
会　云

熊
庶
背
育
些
庞
乘
舌
会
去
允
统

能
燕
北
肯
此
比
乖
古
云
绘
丢
充

Connect the parts of each character by drawing arrows from its first part to its last part. Note some parts are used more than once. Use different coloured arrows for different characters. See examples.

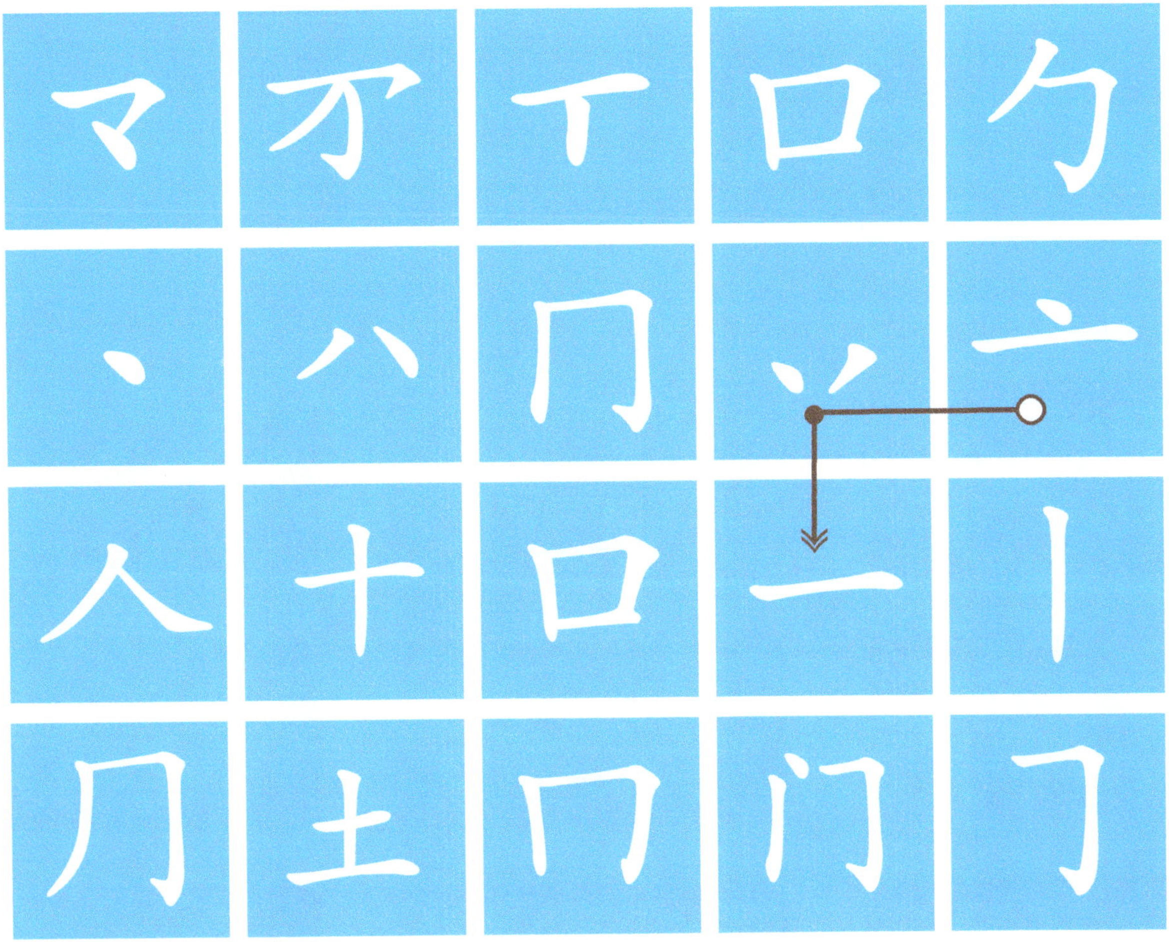

マ	冫	丆	口	勹
丶	八	冂	丷	二
人	十	口	一	丨
刀	土	冂	门	亅

周　尚　高　句　司　同　冋　问　囘　回

闩　令　⟨立⟩　商　商　喬　帚

Activity 82

For some characters, there is more than one way to break down the characters. One of the ways is shown. Think of another way to break it down and colour the parts using the Part Order Colour Code.

These conditions have to be fulfilled:

1. The characters are broken down into qTRAILS alphabets and strokes. Each character has at least one alphabet.

2. The number of parts in each character must be the same.

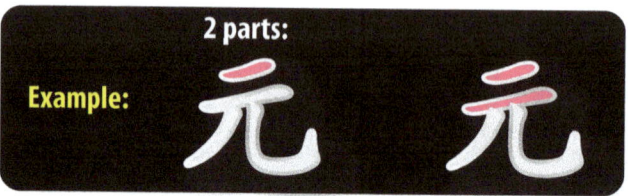

Example: 2 parts: 元　元

午　午　　先　先　　虫　虫

牛　牛　　告　告　　出　出

戈　戈　　乡　乡　　走　走

Part Order
1　2　3　4　5　6

贵 贵　　卡 卡　　击 击

More than 2 ways:

缶 缶 缶　　卯 卯

羌 羌　　甩 甩　　展 展

贱 贱　　竹 竹　　冠 冠

卸 卸　　遣 遣　　寇 寇

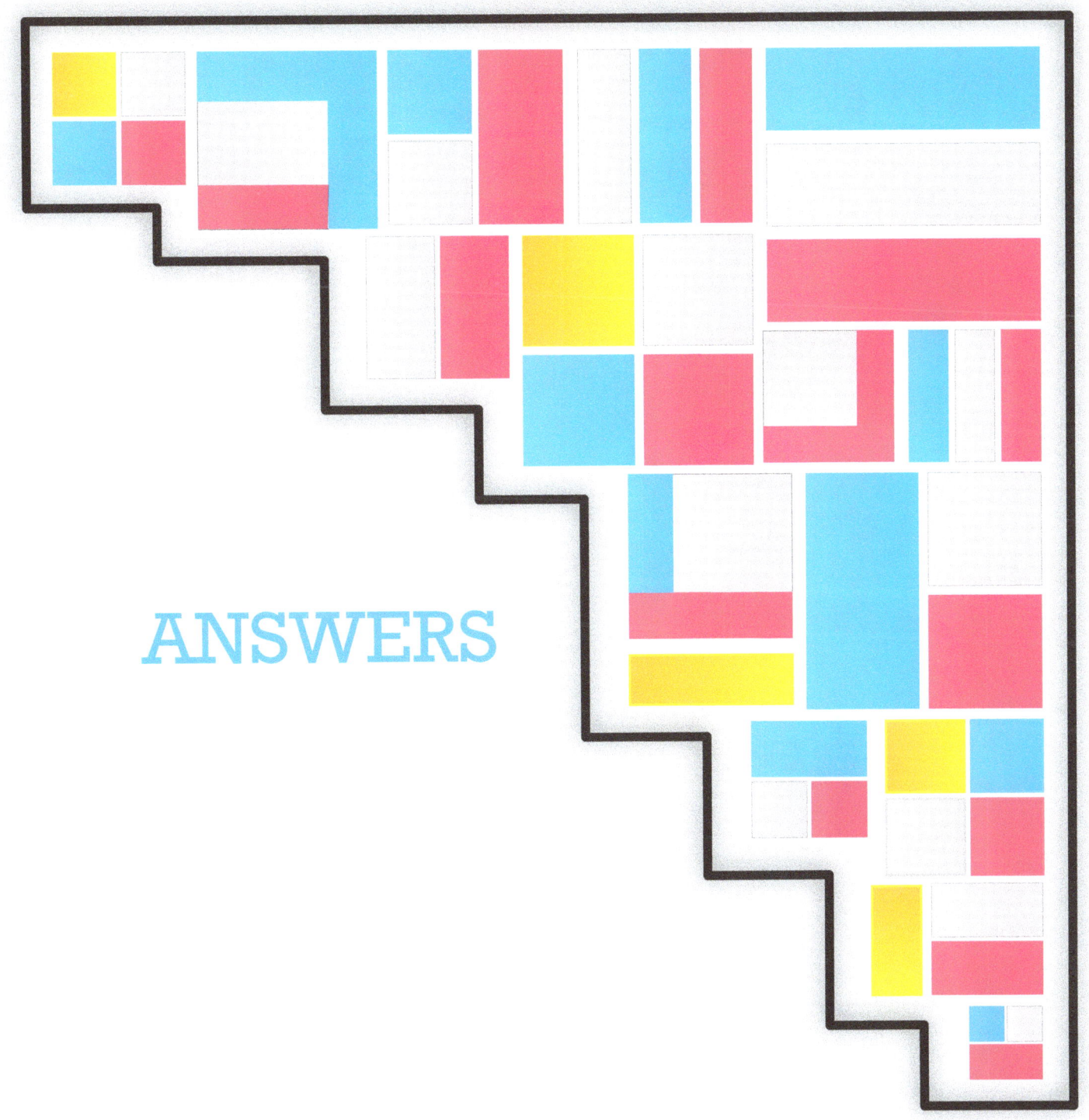

ANSWERS

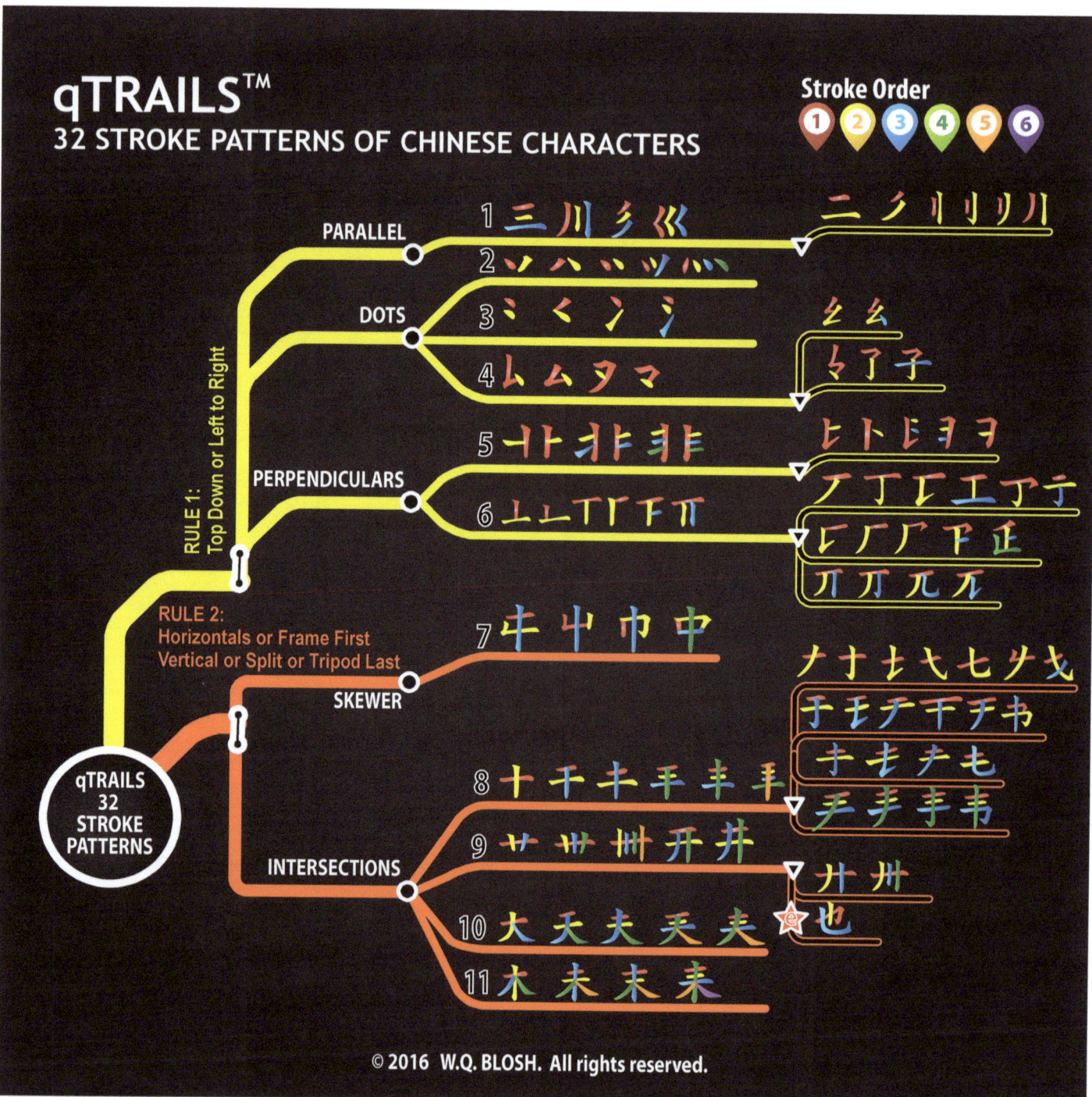

qTRAILS™
32 STROKE PATTERNS OF CHINESE CHARACTERS

qTRAILS 32 STROKE PATTERNS

RULE 3:
Horizontals First
Verticals (Left to Right)
Bottom Horizontal Last

INTERSECTIONS

12 土 王 主 王 业 甚 土 甘 甘 甘 耳

RULE 4:
RL-Slash First &/or
LR-Slash Last

SPLIT & CROSS

13 八 人 入 之 辶
14 亻 彳 亻 勹 勺
15 乀 乀 乀
16 乂 又 廴 孑
17 勹 夕 夂 夊
18 儿 儿 几 九

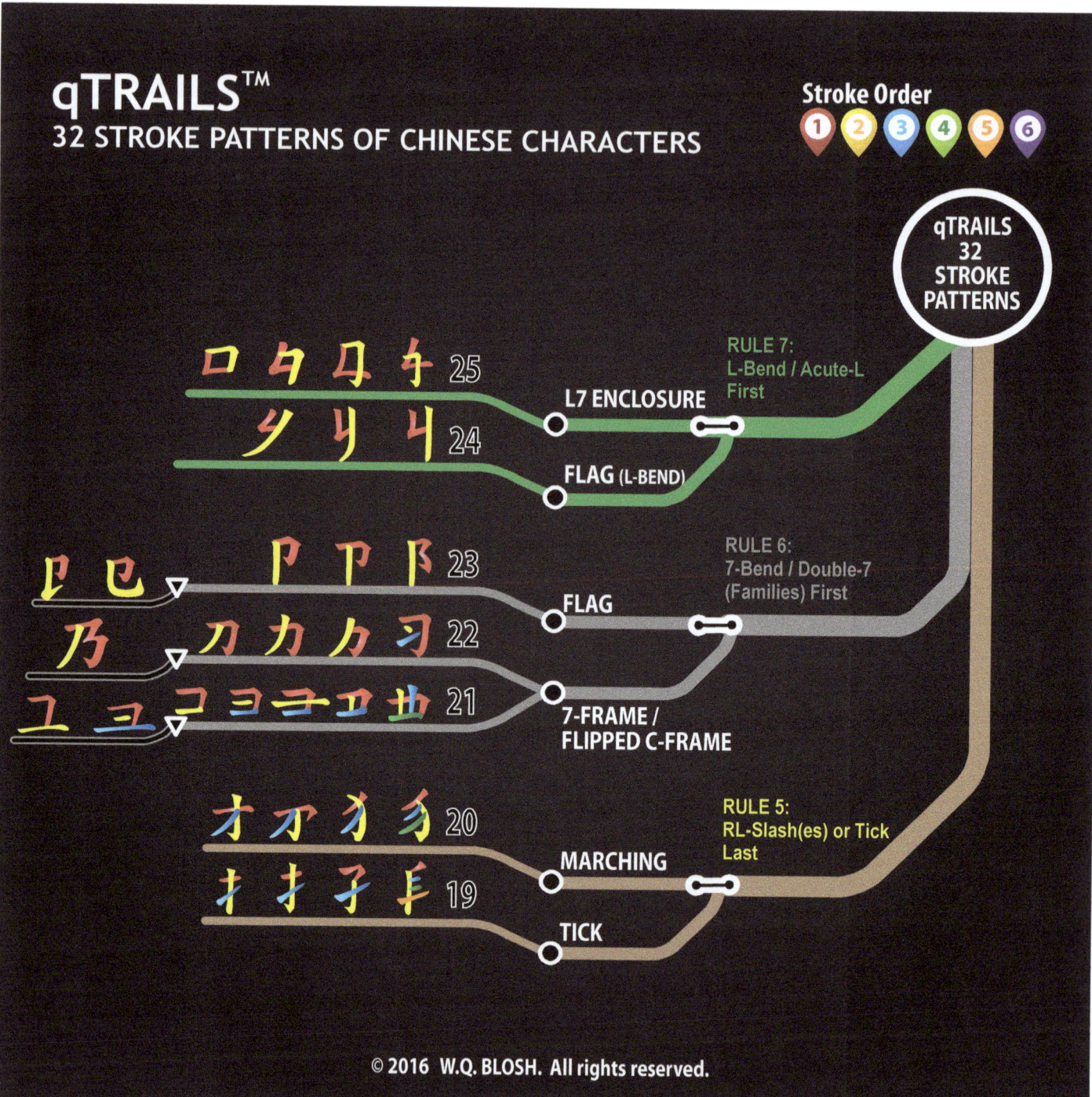

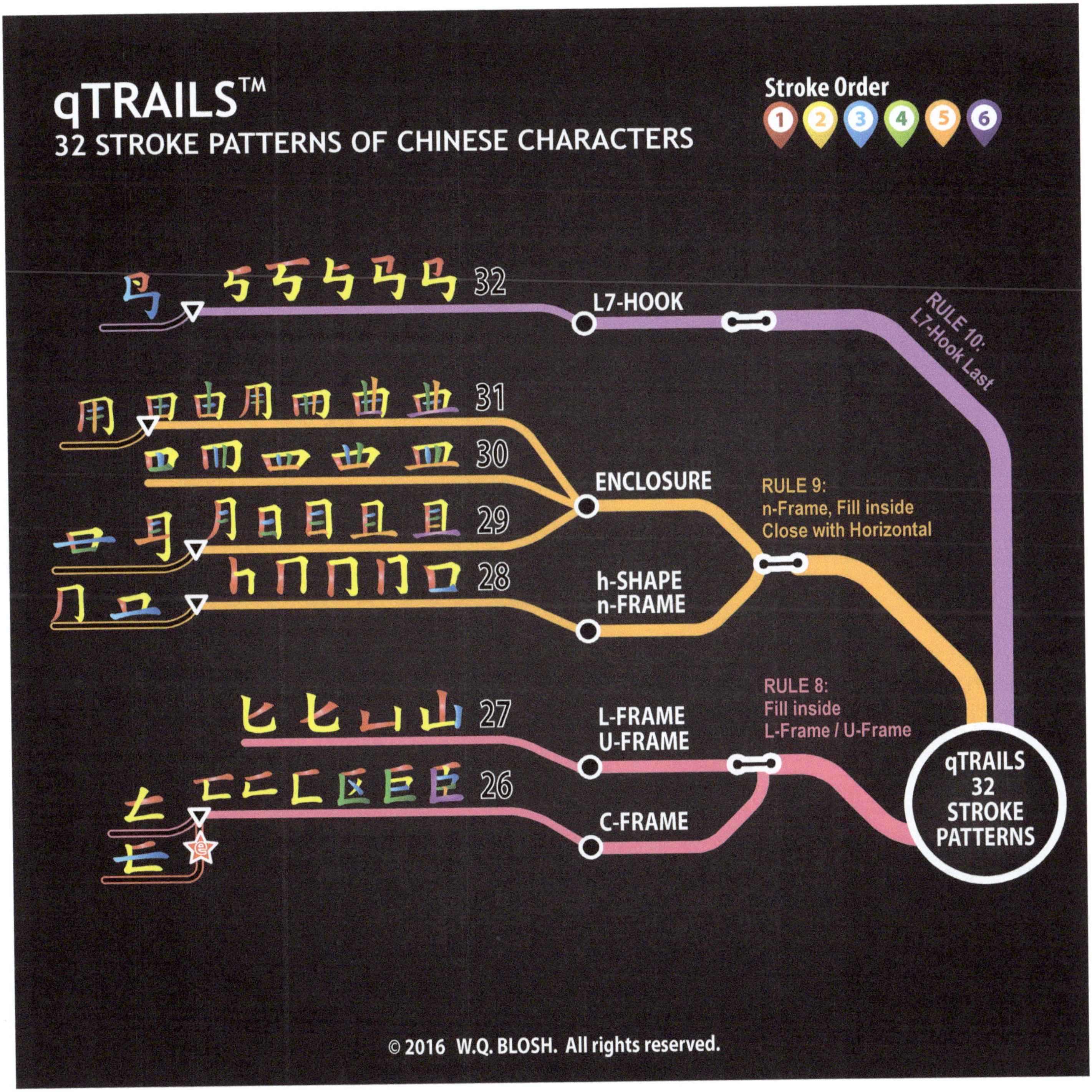

qTRAILS™
32 STROKE PATTERNS OF CHINESE CHARACTERS

马 ㄅ ㄅ ㄅ 马 马 **32**

用 用 由 用 冊 曲 曲 **31**

四 皿 四 曲 皿 **30**

月 月 月 且 且 **29**

ㄐ 口 几 冂 口 **28**

L7-HOOK

ENCLOSURE

**h-SHAPE
n-FRAME**

RULE 9:
n-Frame, Fill inside
Close with Horizontal

匕 匕 凵 山 **27**

亡 匚 匚 匸 区 巨 臣 **26**

**L-FRAME
U-FRAME**

C-FRAME

RULE 8:
Fill inside
L-Frame / U-Frame

**qTRAILS
32
STROKE
PATTERNS**

Activity 1

Activity 2

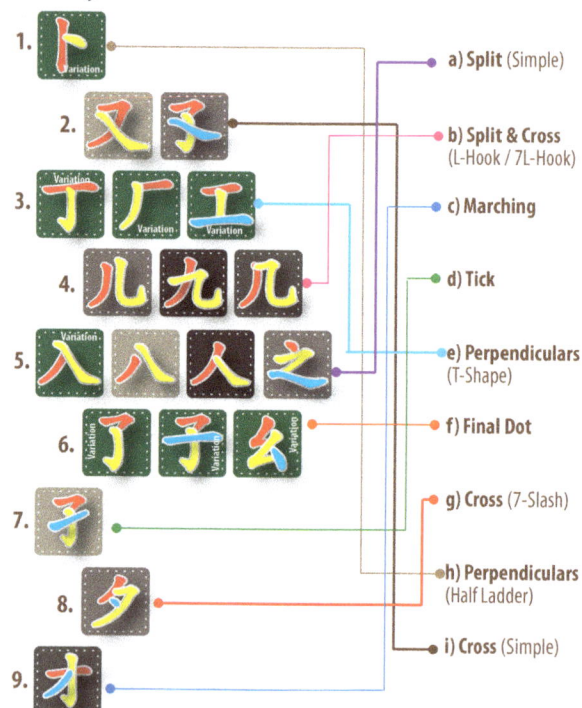

1.
2.
3.
4.
5.
6.
7.
8.
9.

a) **Split** (Simple)

b) **Split & Cross**
(L-Hook / 7L-Hook)

c) **Marching**

d) **Tick**

e) **Perpendiculars**
(T-Shape)

f) **Final Dot**

g) **Cross** (7-Slash)

h) **Perpendiculars**
(Half Ladder)

i) **Cross** (Simple)

Activity 3

a) **L-Frame & U-Frame**

b) **Skewer**

c) **Enclosure**
(Vertical)

d) **7-Hook Frame**

e) **n-Frame /
Enclosure** (Empty)

f) **C-Frame**

g) **Enclosure**
(Horizontal)

h) **Enclosure**
(Intersections)

Activity 4

Activity 5

Activity 6

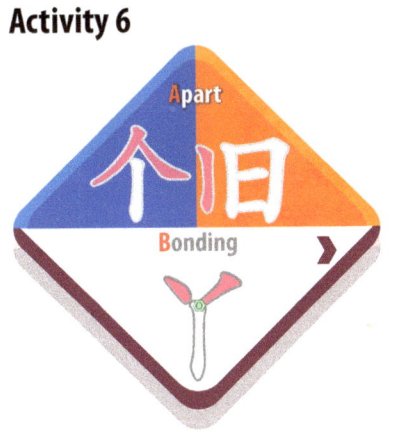

Activity 7

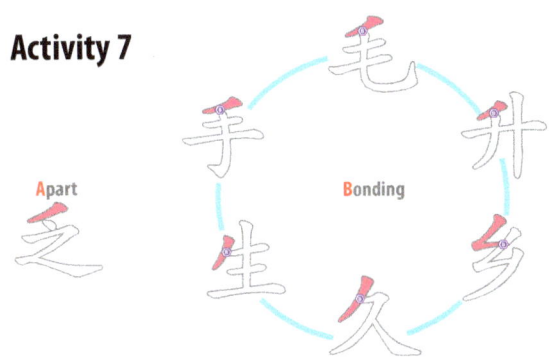

Activity 8

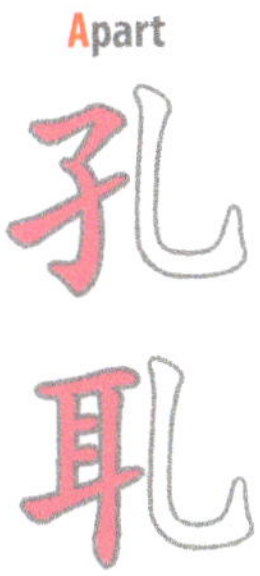

Apart

孔
耻

Activity 9

Activity 10

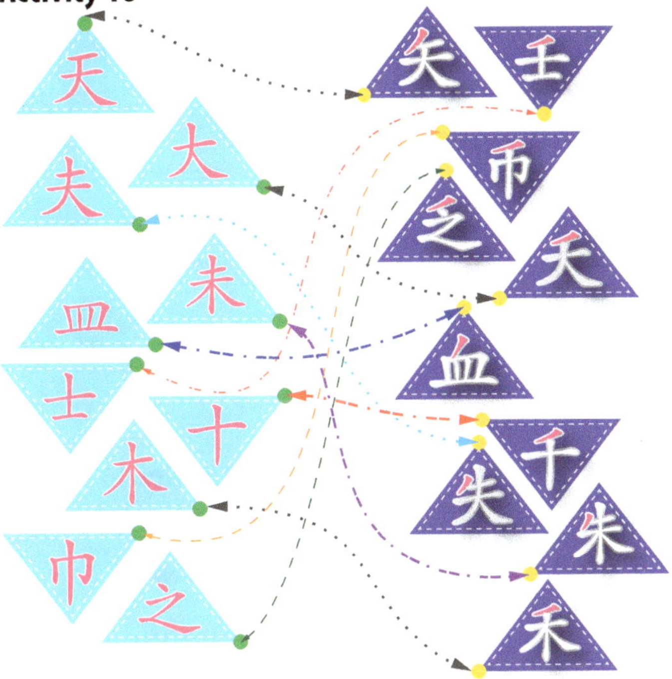

天
夫
大
血
士
木
巾
未
十
之

矢 壬
币
之 天
血
千
失 朱
禾

Activity 11

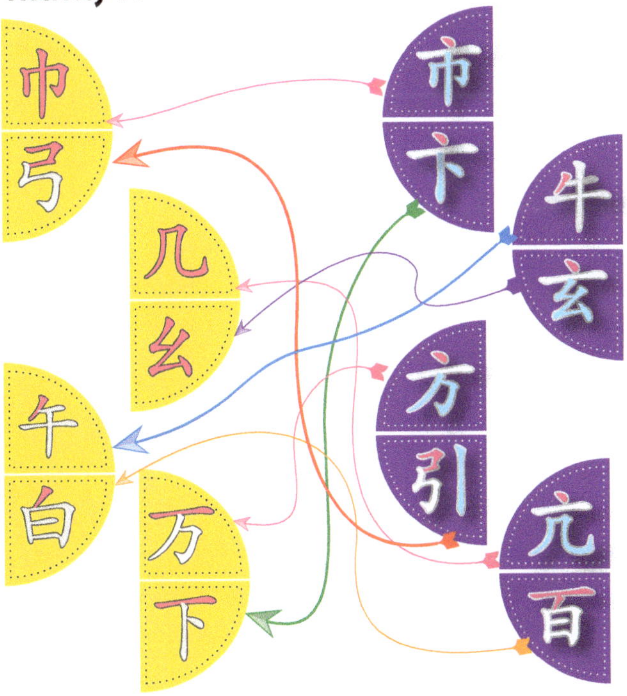

巾
弓
几
幺
午
白
万
下

市
下
牛
玄
方
引
亢
百

Activity 12

文	名	冗	艾	兄
备	父	弄	吞	甾
	奉	介	支	节

Activity 13

肋 卯 巧 昧 仍

叩 归 助 材 刑 枢 幼

Activity 14

卉 奔 具 真

早 覃 卓 罩

而 峏 吕 营

亏 夸 贝 责

Activity 15

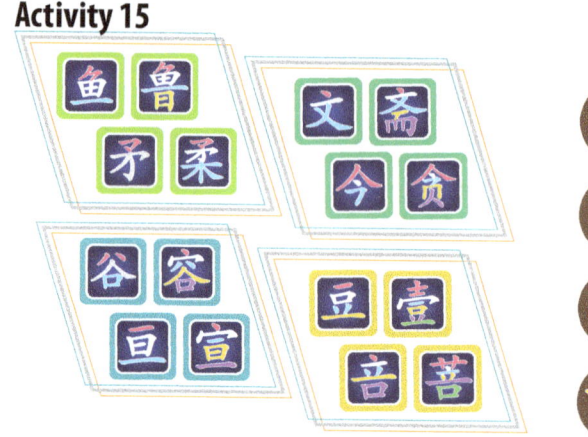

鱼 鲁 矛 柔

文 斋 今 贪

谷 容 亘 宣

豆 壹 音 菩

Activity 16

文 父 爷

玄 畜 蓄

昱 立 音

亡 亡 盲

窦 莫 蒂

帝 帝 蕾

Activity 17

兴 方 它 参 互 宁 查 亼 写 空 基 夏 言 觉 暮 兽

Activity 18

育 章 益 卓 寅 寞 曹 竟

鼻 贲 宁 奚 宽 荒 膏 睿

Activity 19

比 朋 毗 棚 加 耶 咖 椰

相 行 湘 衍 沏 印 切 抑

Activity 20

亿 刊 以 犯 卧 帅 拒 淋

班 耕 排 冲

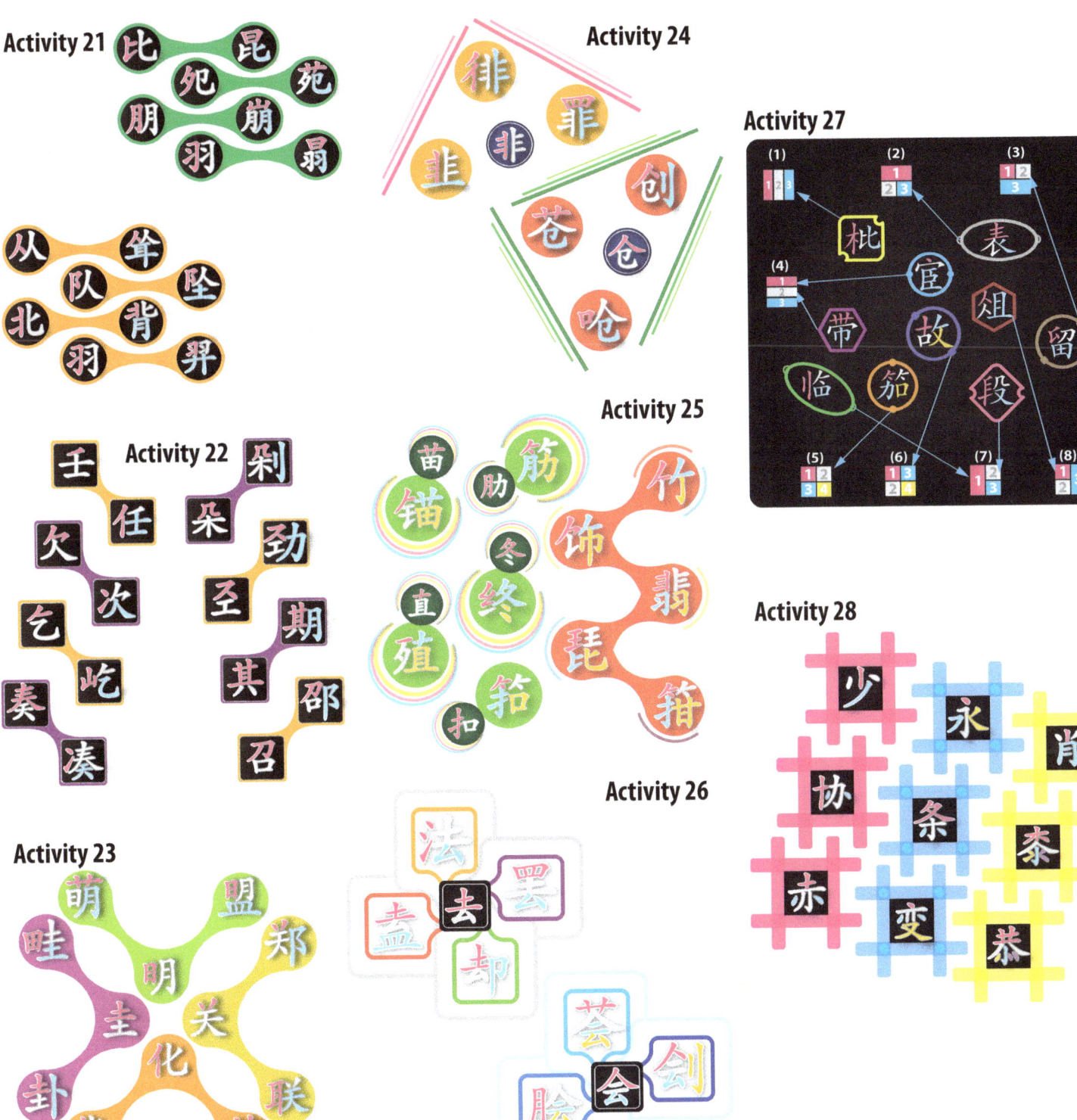

Activity 21

比 昆 兕 苑 朋 崩 羽 扇

从 牟 队 坠 北 背 羽 羿

Activity 24

徘 罪 韭 非 创 仓 仓 呛

Activity 27

(1) 1 2 3
(2) 1 2 3
(3) 1 2 3
枇 表
(4) 1 2 3
宦 俎
带 故 留
临 笛 段
(5) 1 2 3 4
(6) 1 2 3
(7) 1 2
(8) 1 2 3

Activity 22

壬 剁 任 朵 欠 劲 次 至 乞 屹 期 奏 其 凑 邵 召

Activity 25

苗 筋 锚 肋 冬 竹 饰 直 终 翡 殖 笛 琵 扣 箝

Activity 28

少 永 肖 协 条 泰 赤 变 恭

Activity 23

萌 盟 畦 郑 明 圭 关 卦 化 联 华 花

Activity 26

法 显 去 盍 却 荟 会 剑 脍

Activity 29

Activity 30

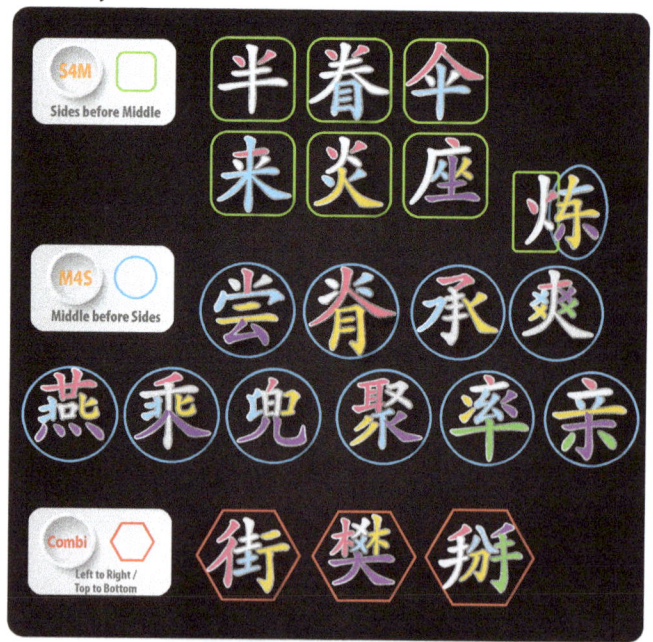

Activity 31

Activity 32

Activity 33

Activity 34

Activity 37

Activity 40

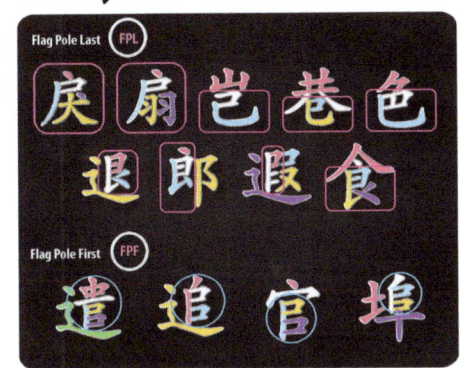

Activity 35

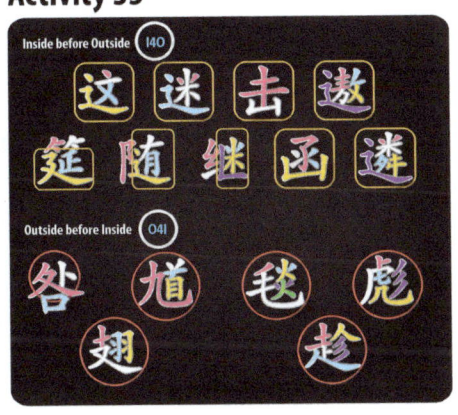

Activity 38

Activity 41

Activity 36

Activity 39

Activity 42

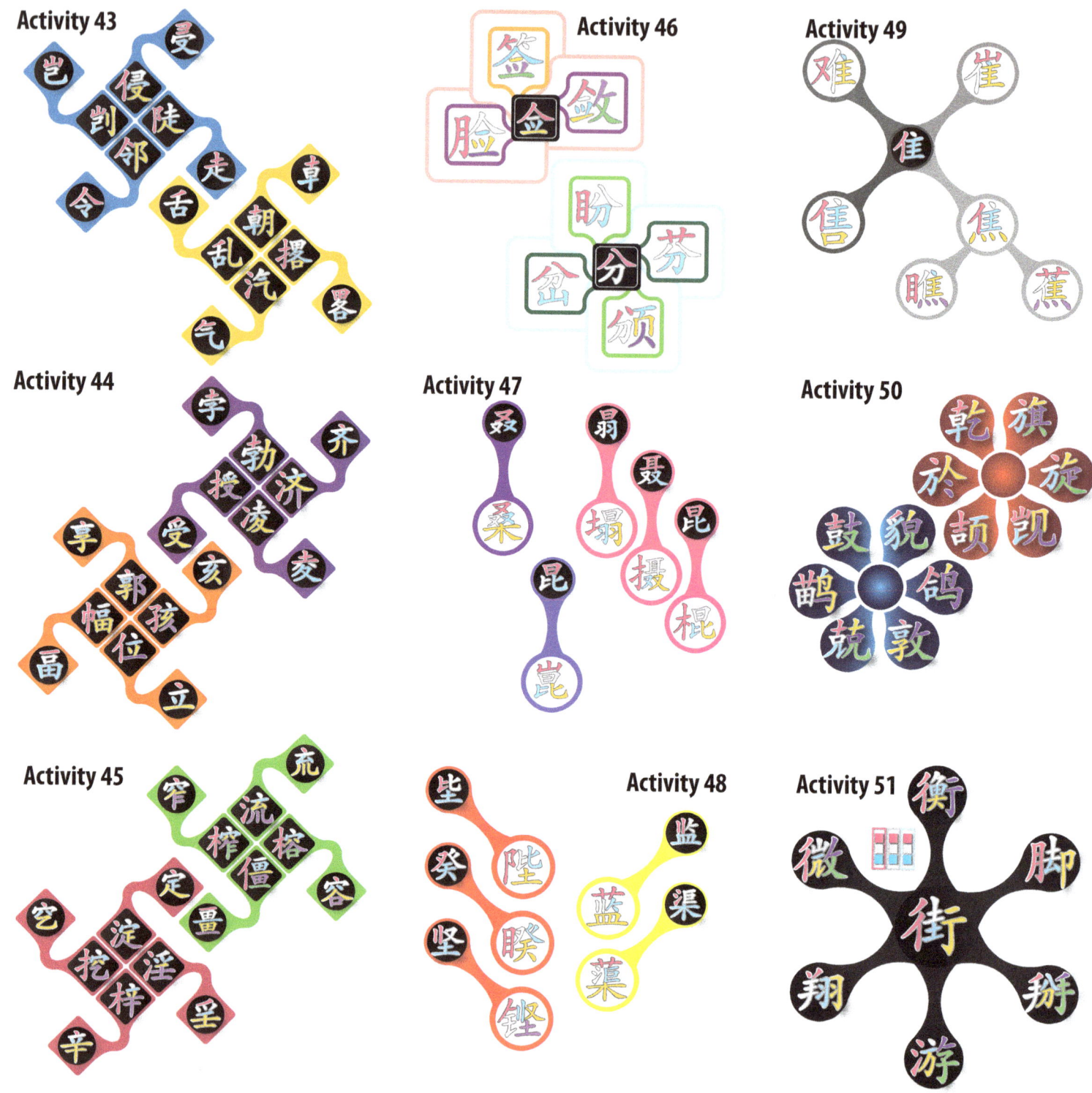

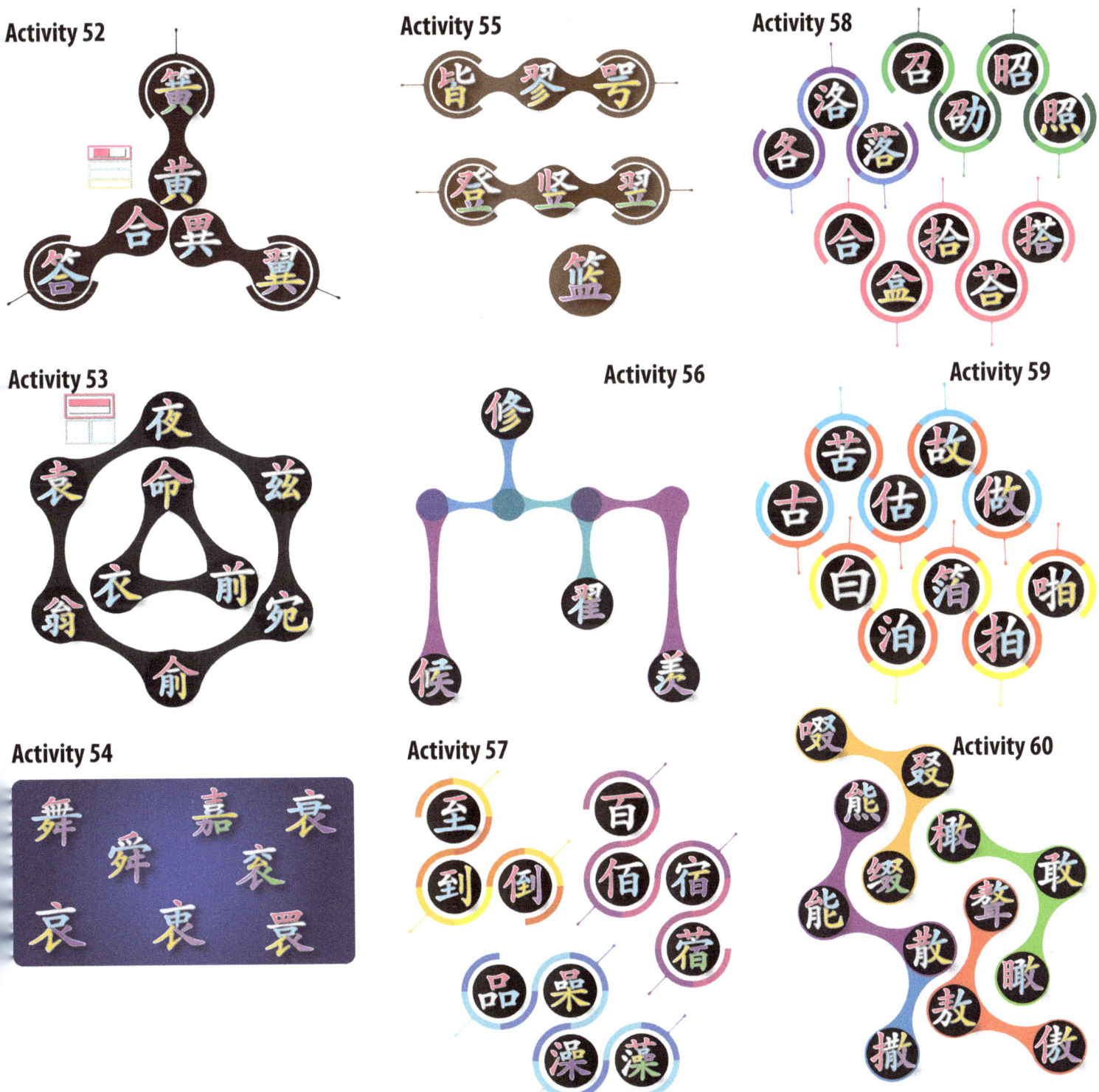

Activity 52

黃 黄 合 異 答 翼

Activity 53

夜 命 茲 袁 衣 前 翁 俞 宛

Activity 54

舞 嘉 哀 舜 衰 哀 衷 裹

Activity 55

皆 琴 罗 登 竪 翌 籃

Activity 56

修 翟 侯 美

Activity 57

至 到 倒 百 佰 宿 宿 品 呆 澡 藻

Activity 58

召 昭 洛 劭 照 各 落 合 拾 搭 盒 荅

Activity 59

苦 故 古 估 做 白 箔 啪 泊 拍

Activity 60

啜 叕 熊 橄 缀 敢 能 聲 散 瞰 敖 撒 傲

Activity 61

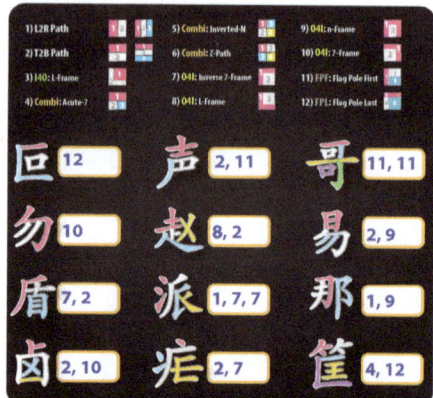

Activity 62

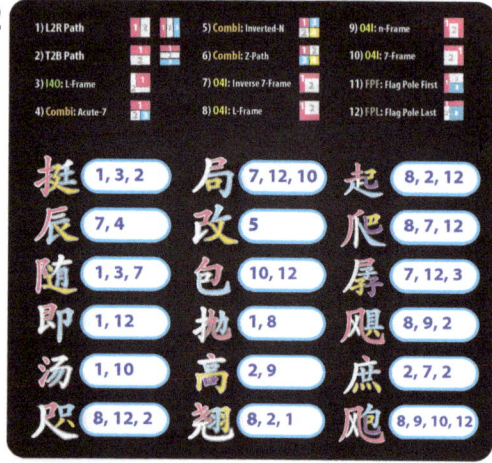

Activity 63

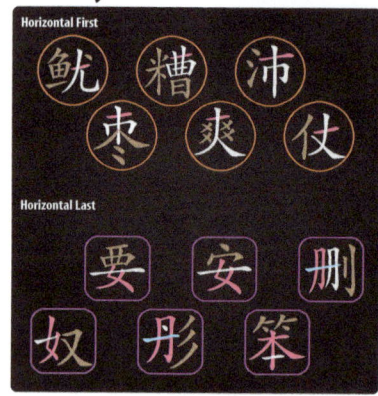

Activity 64

Activity 65

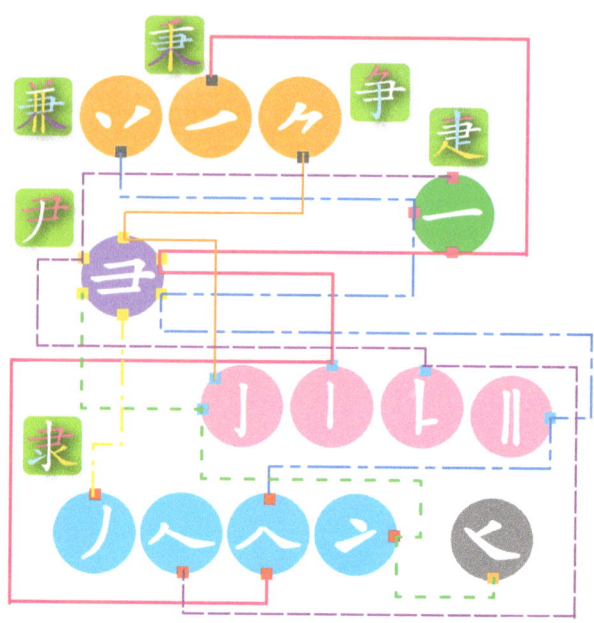

Activity 66

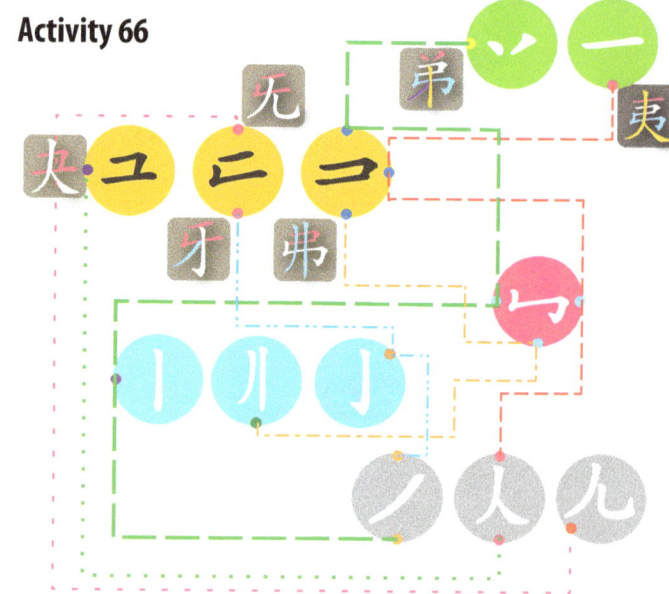

Activity 67

课 | ☑ 丶讠曰木 ☐ 丶讠田木
建 | ☐ 彐十廴 ☑ 彐十廴
陆 | ☑ 阝二山 ☐ 阝土山
量 | ☑ 田一曰土 ☐ 田一田土
妾 | ☑ 丶丷二女一 ☐ 丶丷二女

匣 | ☑ 一日匚 ☐ 一田匚
蜣 | ☐ 口丷𠃌九 ☑ 口丷三九
屈 | ☑ 尸凵山 ☐ 尸凵山
使 | ☐ 亻十口乂 ☑ 亻一口乂
饶 | ☑ 饣戈口九灬 ☐ 饣戈口九灬

Activity 68

耦 | ☑ 耒日冂小 ☐ 耒田冂小
软 | ☑ 一中八入 ☐ 十口八入
象 | ☑ 𠂊口豕乀 ☐ 𠂊四豕乀
棘 | ☐ 十八中八 ☑ 十八一八
逆 | ☑ 丷一屮辶 ☐ 丷一山辶

專 | ☑ 一口小寸 ☐ 一田小寸
重 | ☐ 一十田土 ☑ 一一曰土
魅 | ☐ 日儿厶未 ☐ 田儿厶未
禹 | ☑ 一口冂小 ☐ 一田冂小
妻 | ☐ 十彐女一 ☑ 一彐乂一

Activity 69

龟 筮 宴
再 波 军
身 缸 更
农 酉 老

Activity 70

长 年 丑 我
孝 武 白 量

Activity 71

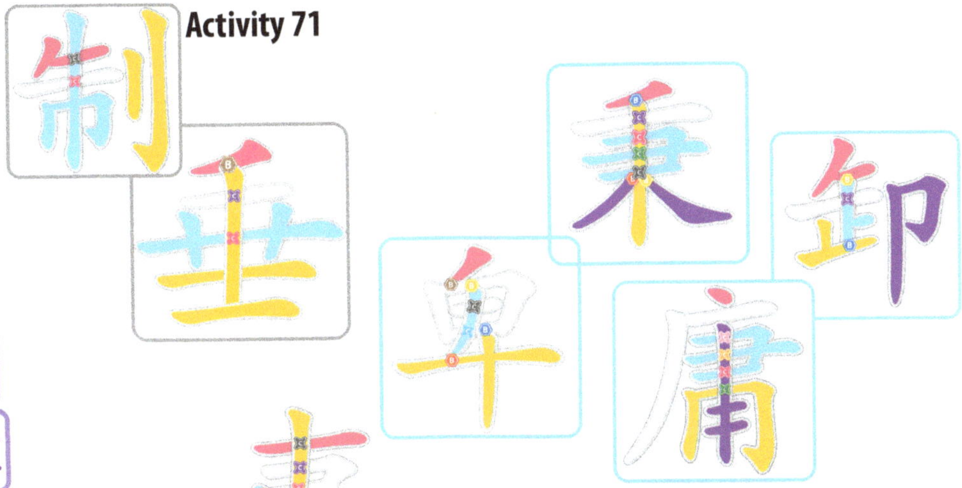

制 垂 卑 秉 卸 庸
夷 第 藏 鼎

Activity 72

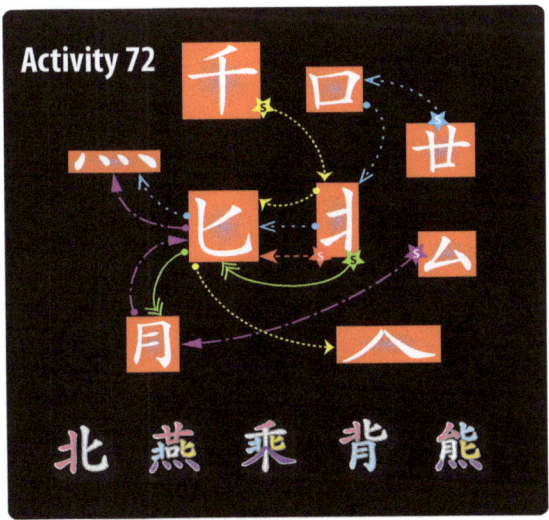

千 口 廿 宀 匕 且 厶 月 入

北 燕 乘 背 熊

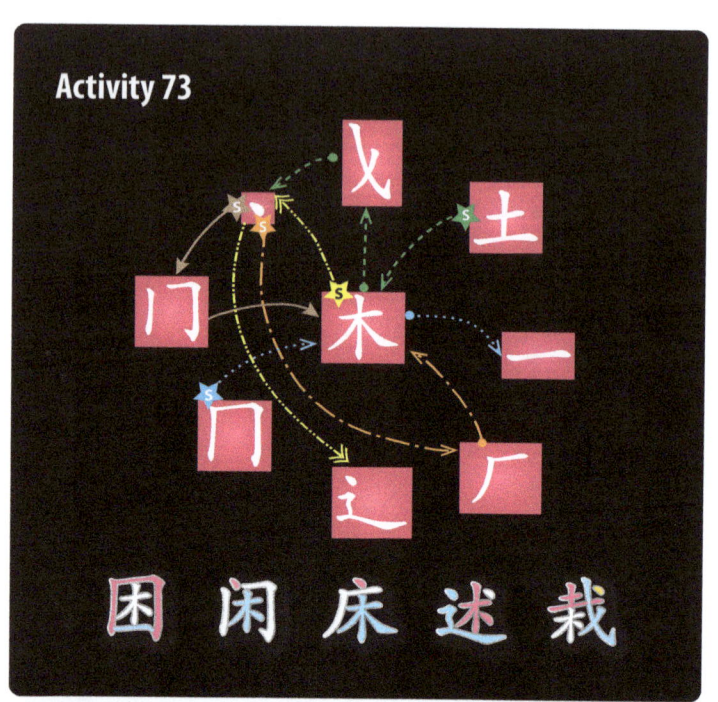

Activity 73

困 闲 床 述 栽

Activity 75

臧 鼎 寐

Activity 74

卧 宦 拒 臧 渠

Activity 76

迷 继 渊 类 断

| 1, 5 | 7, 1, 4 | 6, 2, 3, 1 | 1, 8 | 1, 4, 9 |

Activity 77

凶	冈	区	囟	赵
1, 7, 3	3, 6, 1	10, 1, 7	11, 3, 5, 1, 10	8, 12, 9, 1
卤	网	风	卤	匈
2, 10, 1, 7, 3	3, 6, 1, 1	11, 4, 1	12, 3, 5, 1, 10	11, 6, 1, 7, 3

Activity 78

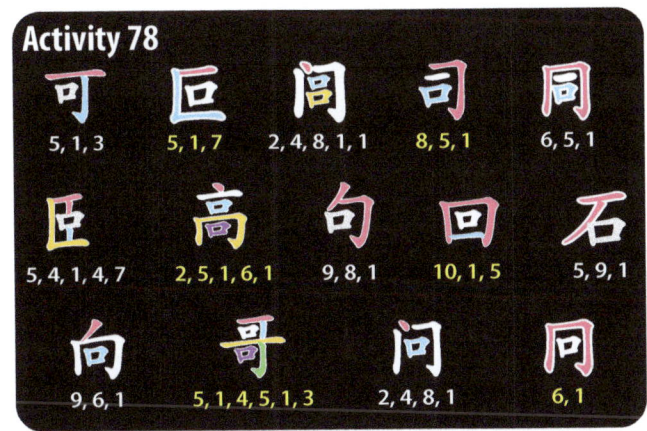

可	匠	同	司	同
5, 1, 3	5, 1, 7	2, 4, 8, 1, 1	8, 5, 1	6, 5, 1
臣	高	句	回	石
5, 4, 1, 4, 7	2, 5, 1, 6, 1	9, 8, 1	10, 1, 5	5, 9, 1
向	哥	问	同
9, 6, 1	5, 1, 4, 5, 1, 3	2, 4, 8, 1	6, 1

Activity 79

户	民	所	段
5, 1, 2	1, 17, 14	9, 1, 9, 12	1, 18, 1, 13
启	局	官	卣
5, 1, 2, 6	1, 2, 8, 6	5, 16, 3, 1, 1	11, 10, 1, 4
卢	巴	巨	臣
11, 1, 2	1, 15	4, 1, 7	12, 1, 3, 7

Activity 81

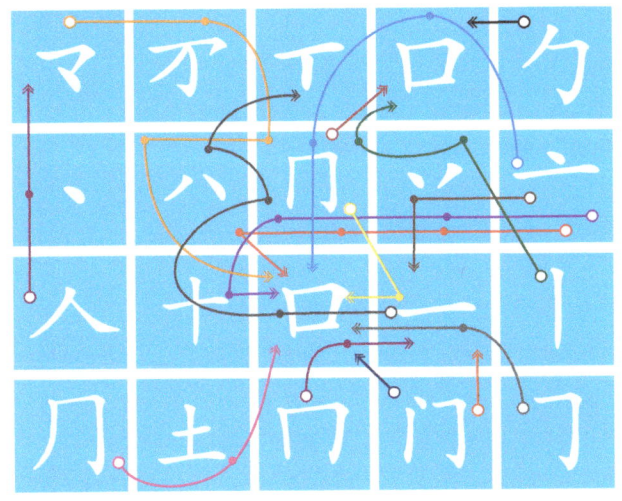

Activity 80

Activity 82

午午	先先	虫虫
牛牛	告告	出出
戈戈	乡乡	走走

贵贵	卡卡	击击
缶缶缶		卯卯
羌羌	甩甩	展展
贱贱	竹竹	冠冠
卸卸	遣遣	寇寇

APPLYING WHAT YOU'VE LEARNT

Characters With More Than 6 Parts

You have come to the end of the book. Did you realise that you have only seen characters up to 6 parts. What about characters with more than 6 parts?

Most of the characters with more than 6 parts are created by combining simple characters or parts using two or more basic structures.

As such, we do not want to introduce characters with very complex structures (7 or more parts) in this book, which will make learning characters confusing. We would recommend that you become very proficient in dissecting characters with basic structures first and apply concepts you learnt in the section on *Simple to Complex* to decode these charcters.

Many Ways to Decode Characters Visually

As shown in the activity 'Dual Ways', you can see that for some characters there is more than one way to deconstruct, that is different parts can be extracted from the same character but the Part Order of the character remains the same.

Deviations

In this series of books, we have also deliberately deferred from the Stroke Order Guidelines provided by academic bodies on a few characters. This is to make them conform to existing rules better and hence easier to remember.

Redefinition

We seek to redefine the composition of Chinese characters through the introduction of qTRAILS

80/20 - Mostly T2B or L2R

When decoding Chinese characters you will be applying the first two rules of Standard Part Order most of the time:

> Rule 1: Top to Bottom (T2B) or Left to Right (L2R) and
>
> Rule 2: A combination of T2B and L2R

Most characters are written this way.

Don't See Characters in Strokes

By now, you would have learnt not to see characters in individual strokes, but

> see **characters with simple structures** in **PARTS** (alphabets or strokes)
>
> see **characters with complex structures** in **SIMPLE CHARACTERS** and **PARTS**

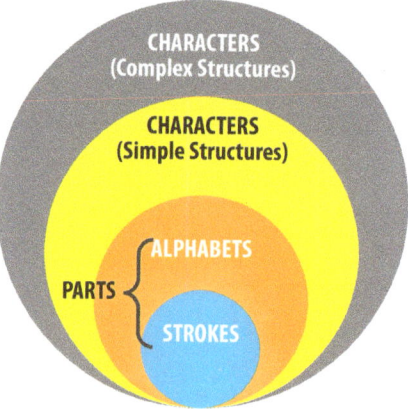

Alphabets, 35 Strokes and new concepts like Triple ABCs Concepts (e.g. Apart, Bonding, Crossing, Adaptation).

In other words, we provide you with another pair of lenses to observe and appreciate Chinese characters. This is just one way of seeing, an easier way to visualise and remember the few thousands frequently-used simplified characters.

Learn Chinese *without* WRITING

Chinese Strokes Book

Chinese Alphabets Book

Chinese Spelling Book

Scan this QR code to get LCWW1

Scan this QR code to get LCWW2

Learn Chinese *without* WRITING *For Kids*

Scan this QR code to get LCWWFK1

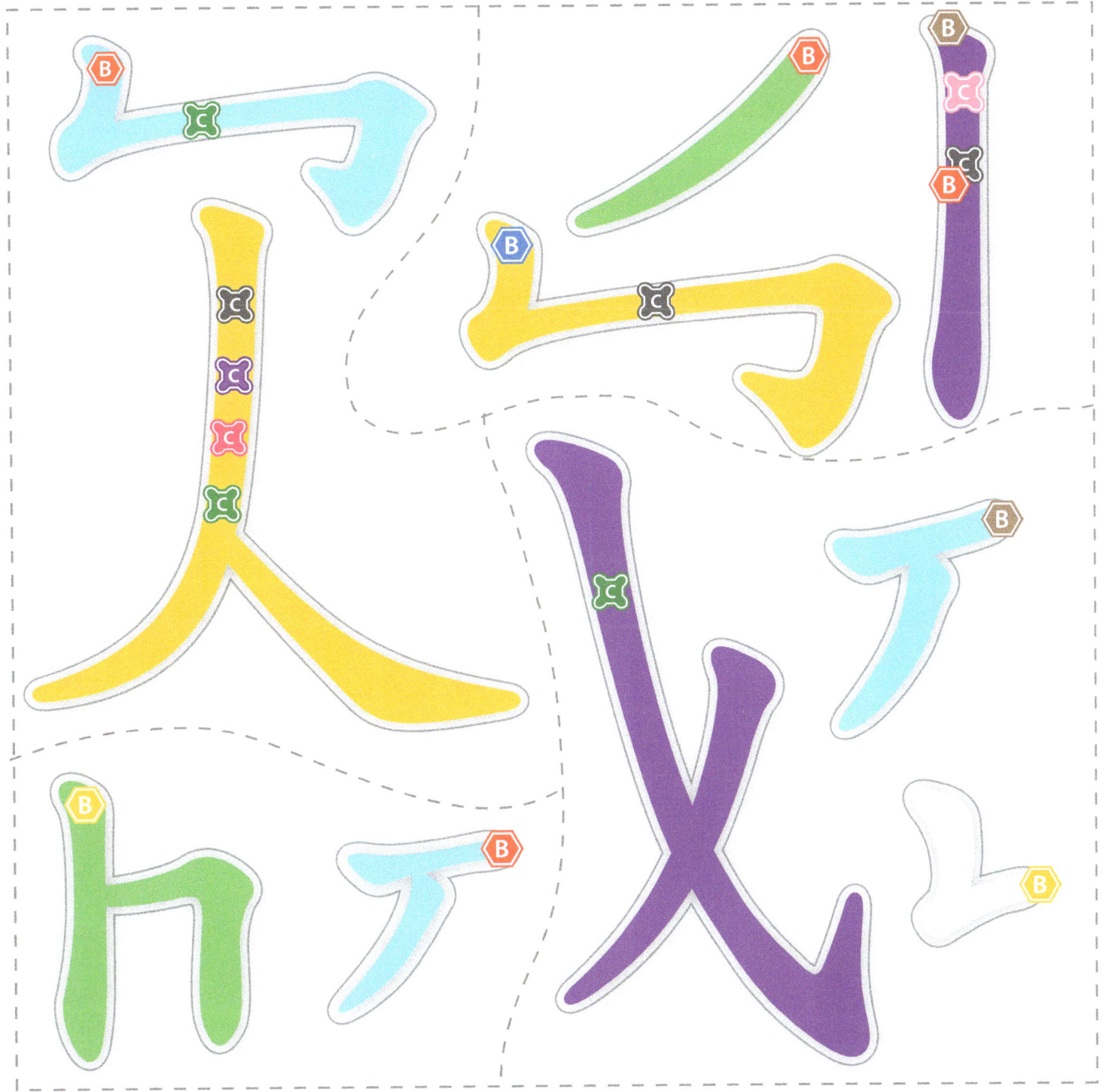

Cut out the parts along the grey outlines of each part.

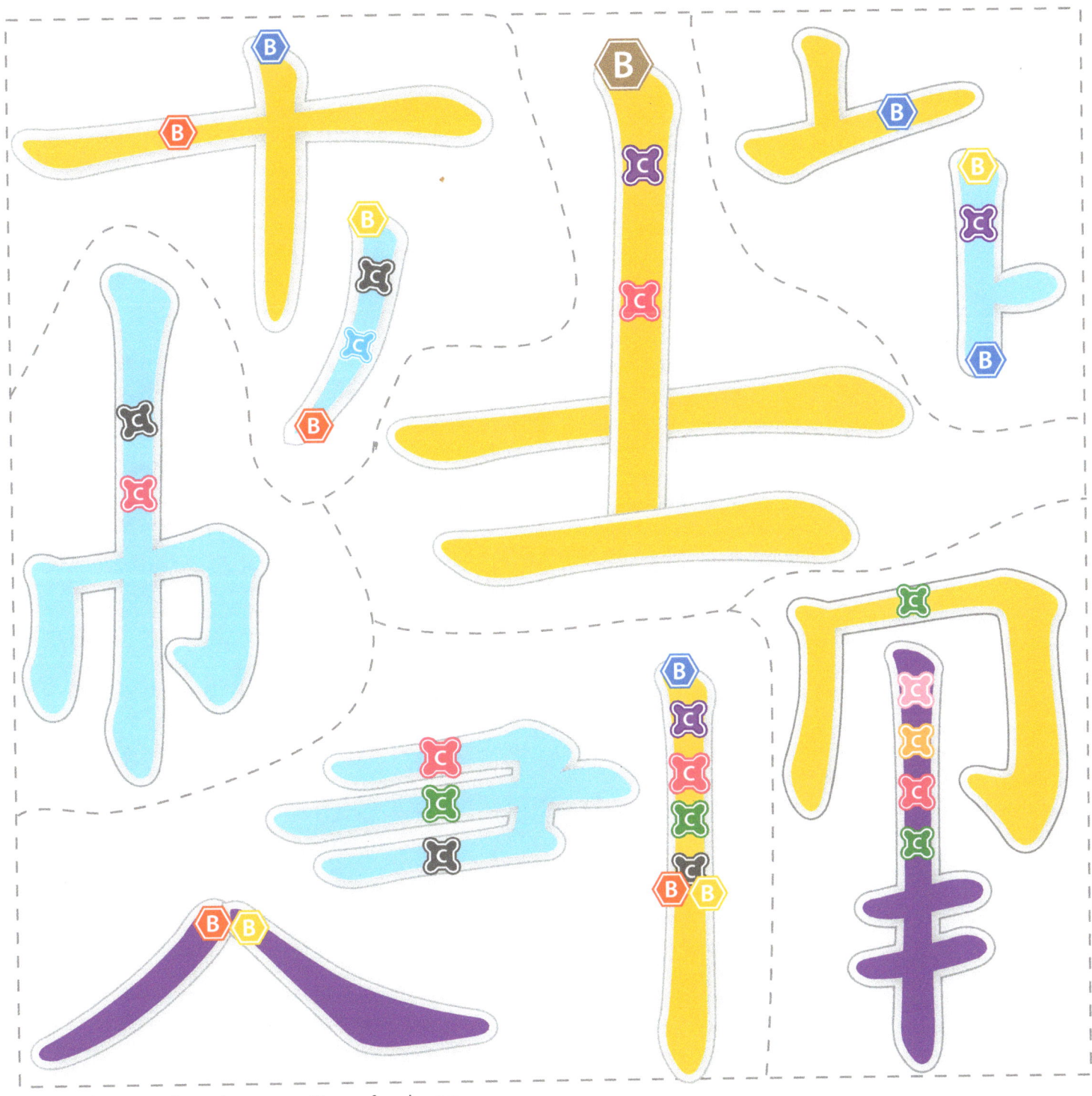

Cut out the parts along the grey outlines of each part.

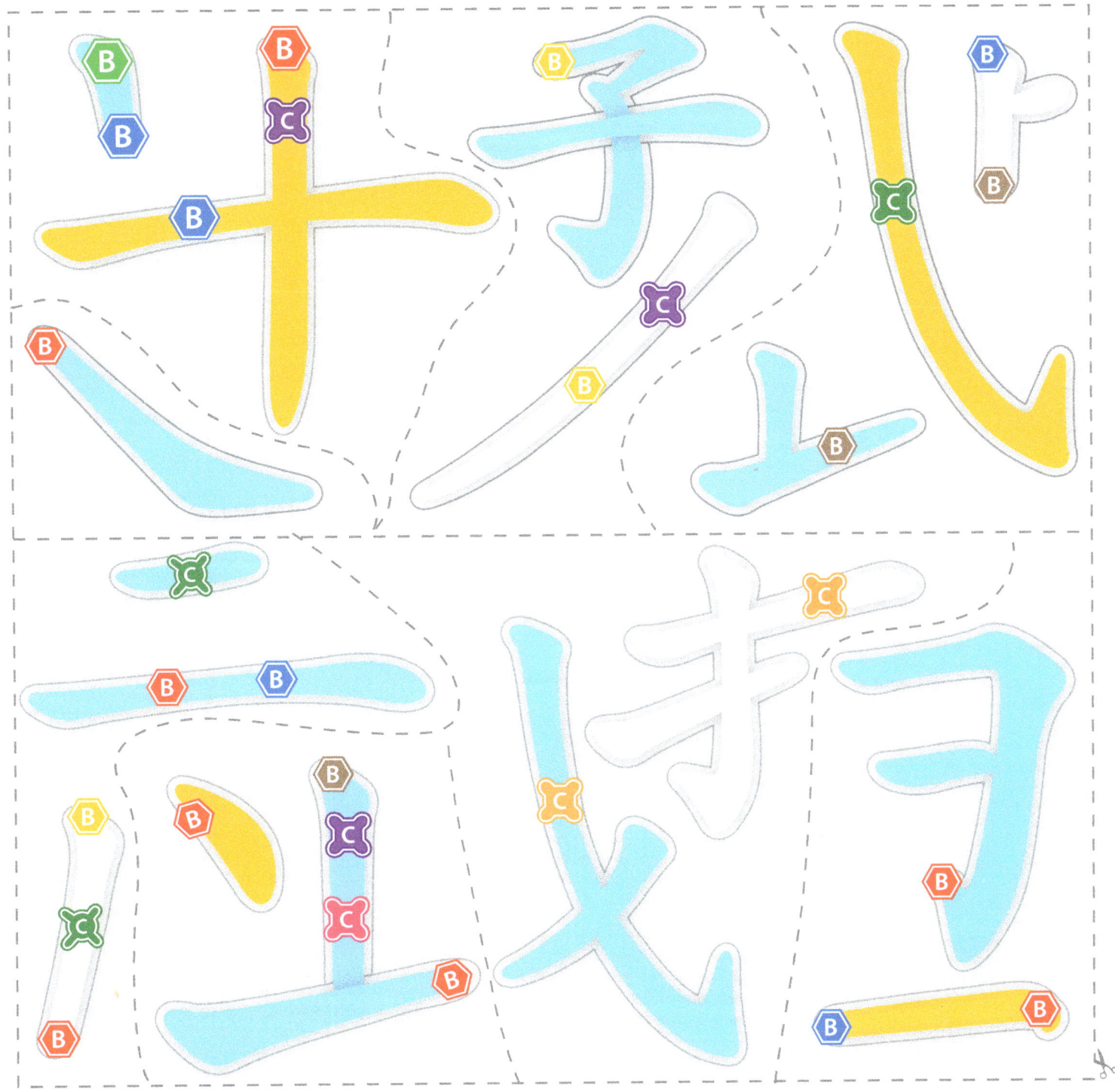

Cut out the parts along the grey outlines of each part.

Cut out these basic alphabets and paste into the correct qTRAILS in RECAP section.

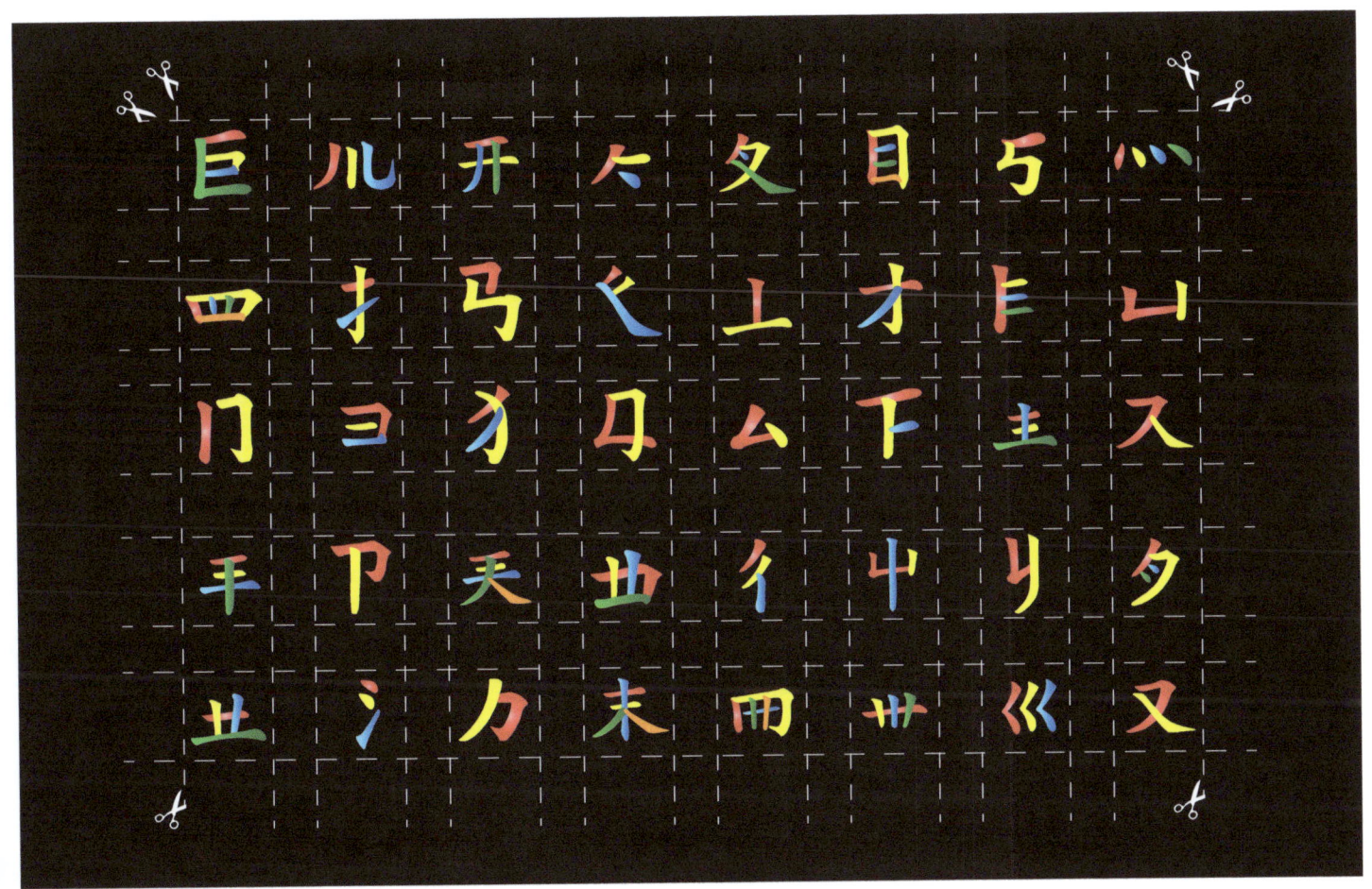

www.ingramcontent.com/pod-product-compliance
Lightning Source LLC
Chambersburg PA
CBHW041112120626
46547CB00019B/2680